COMPLETE GUIDE
TO
TRUST ACCOUNTING
AND
TRUST INCOME TAXATION

COMPLETE GUIDE TO

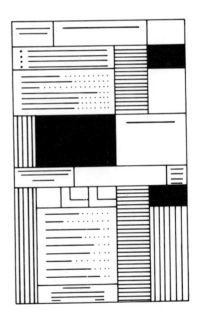

TRUST ACCOUNTING
AND
TRUST INCOME TAXATION

J.G. Denhardt, Jr. CPA

with

James W. Denhardt, J.D.

PRENTICE-HALL, INC.   Englewood Cliffs, N.J.

Complete Guide to Trust Accounting
and Trust Income Taxation
by
J.G. Denhardt, Jr. CPA
with
James W. Denhardt, J.D.

Prentice-Hall International, Inc., *London*
Prentice-Hall of Australia, Pty. Ltd., *Sydney*
Prentice-Hall of Canada, Ltd., *Toronto*
Prentice-Hall of India Private Ltd., *New Delhi*
Prentice-Hall of Japan, Inc., *Tokyo*
Prentice-Hall of Southeast Asia Pte. Ltd., *Singapore*
Whitehall Books, Ltd., *Wellington, New Zealand*

Library of Congress Cataloging in Publication Data

Denhardt, J.G.
    Complete guide to trust accounting and trust income
taxation.

    Includes index.
    1. Trusts and trustees--United States. 2. Trusts
and trustees--Accounting. 3. Trusts and trustees--
Taxation--United States. I. Denhardt, James W., joint
author. II. Title.
HG4495.U5D46   657'.833   77-5855
ISBN 0-13-160739-1

Printed in the United States of America

ABOUT THE AUTHORS

Member of the American Institute of CPA's and the Kentucky Society of CPA's, J.G. Denhardt, Jr. has held positions as staff accountant with Arthur Andersen & Co. of Chicago, chief auditor with the Kentucky Unemployment Compensation Commission, accountant on the staff of Albert B. Maloney & Co. of Nashville, Tennessee, and auditor for Lampkin Hotel Company, Bowling Green, Kentucky.

Since 1959 he has served as executor of the C.W. Lampkin Estate and has been an individual practitioner in Bowling Green, Kentucky. He has also taught accounting and taxation at Western Kentucky University on a part-time basis since 1946.

Mr. Denhardt has served as discussion leader a number of times for professional development courses for accountants in the estate field, and he is the author of "Complete Guide to Estate Accounting and Taxes," published by Prentice-Hall, Inc.

He is presently a member and Secretary of the Kentucky State Board of Accountancy.

He was graduated with a B.S. Degree from Western Kentucky University in 1935 and received his B.S. in Accounting from Bowling Green College of Commerce in 1936. He resides in Bowling Green, Kentucky.

* * *

James W. Denhardt is a practicing attorney and a partner in a law firm in St. Petersburg, Florida. He is a member of the Florida Bar Association.

Mr. Denhardt was graduated from Western Kentucky University in 1968, receiving a B.S. Degree in Accounting. After serving a term in the military service, he attended the Stetson University School of Law in St. Petersburg, Florida, and was awarded the degree of Juris Doctor.

He served as a prosecuting attorney with the Florida State Attorney's office for several years before going into private practice.

A WORD FROM
THE AUTHORS

The use of trusts is becoming increasingly popular in family financial planning and in tax planning. Traditionally, trusts have been associated with great fortunes, yet many people of ordinary means have discovered that trusts are a convenient legal device to help dispose of assets, reduce taxes, and solve more commonplace financial problems.

Trusts are not new; they have been used for many, many years. But in most sections of our country financial, estate, and tax planners have not until rather recently started taking advantage of this excellent device for saving taxes and for accomplishing many other different desirable objectives.

There is no denying that the use of trusts can be quite complicated, and there is general agreement that the taxation of trusts is one of the more difficult areas of taxation. But it is no more difficult to become familiar with trusts in general and their taxation in particular than with many other phases of planning and taxation the average practitioner must know, and this book includes all the information a person needs to acquire this familiarity.

For the accountant, there is a section describing the accounting system for a trust, including the step-by-step procedures for setting up the general ledger accounts, for making the opening entry and the entries for each transaction, and for preparing the periodic reports. Each step is explained and illustrated in detail, with the reasons for, and the reasoning behind, each step.

For the accountant, lawyer, trust officer, and even the individual trustee who needs to become more familiar with the income taxation of trusts, there is a section describing this in complete detail. Simple tools are given for gathering the necessary figures and for correctly transferring them to the tax return. Many illustrations and examples are included to help make the requirements and procedures more easily understood. The tax law's requirements are given for each step, including those of the Tax Reform Act of 1976 affecting trust taxation.

And for anyone interested in having a better understanding of trusts in general and their uses and tax-planning potential, there is a section of background information about trusts. This section should be interesting and helpful to the reader though not absolutely essential to an understanding of trust accounting or taxation.

This book will answer many questions which might arise in the mind of a practitioner who is not a specialist in trust work, such as:

Who pays the tax on trust income?

What is the difference between trust accounting and ordinary accounting?

Should a trust provide for depreciation in its accounts?

What is a marital deduction trust?

How can the use of a trust save income taxes?

Did the Tax Reform Act of 1976 completely eliminate the use of trusts as an estate tax saving tool?

What are the five steps in arriving at a trust's taxable income?

How and when is a beneficiary taxed on a trust's income?

What is the proper form for a trust report to the court?

What are a trustee's duties and responsibilities?

What tax year must be used by a trust?

What is meant by fiduciary accounting income?

Is there a simple worksheet for use in arriving at a trust's tax return figures?

How does the termination of a trust affect its taxation?

What is the "throwback rule?"

How much did the Tax Reform Act of 1976 affect trust taxation?

These and many other questions are answered in detail in this book, which includes all the essential information about trusts and their accounting and taxation needed to lead a practitioner into an interesting, new, lucrative area of practice and to make him much more expert and at ease when working in this field.

We would like to express our appreciation to Prentice-Hall, Inc., for granting permission to make use of their published materials, particularly *Complete Guide to Estate Accounting and Taxes* and *Federal Tax Guide 1976*; to the American Institute of CPA's for the use of their manual for the seminar on *Income Taxation of Estates and Trusts;* and to Gilbert Law Summaries for permission to make use of their excellent summary. *Trusts.*

J.G. Denhardt, Jr.

James W. Denhardt

CONTENTS

2. **THE KINDS OF TRUSTS** (cont.)

3. **THE TRUSTEE'S DUTIES AND RESPONSIBILITIES**

**A COMPLETE TRUST ACCOUNTING CASE
STUDY ILLUSTRATED** (cont.)

COMPLETE GUIDE
TO
TRUST ACCOUNTING
AND
TRUST INCOME TAXATION

1

INTRODUCTION
TO TRUSTS

The trust has been called the crowning achievement of Anglo-American law. It is the most flexible method known for disposing of property, either temporarily or permanently. Its flexibility is limited only by the imaginations of the property owner and the draftsman of the trust instrument.

A valuable tool of this kind can have many beneficial uses in family financial planning, in estate planning, and in tax planning in general, and a familiarity with trusts and their uses is vital to financial and tax planners, such as lawyers, accountants, and trust officers.

A good working knowledge of trusts includes not only how to handle a trust's accounting system and its income taxation but some background knowledge about trusts in general. While this general information about trusts and a full knowledge of all trusts is not essential in connection with the accounting and taxation of trusts, several chapters of such background will certainly be of interest and help to someone seeking to be well informed on trusts.

WHAT IS A TRUST?

A trust is a fiduciary relationship in which one person holds the legal title to certain property, and another person has the equitable, or beneficial, ownership of the property. The holder of the legal title is known as a trustee, and he has an equitable obligation to keep or use that property interest for the benefit of another, known as a beneficiary.

There are, therefore, two forms of ownership in the same property at the same time, one legal, the other equitable.

A trust might also be defined as a person's right, enforceable in courts of equity, to the beneficial enjoyment of property (such as the income from it), the legal title to which is held by another.

A trust can generally be created only by a person who owns property, and it is created when that person either expressly or impliedly transfers that property to another with specifications and restrictions as to the use to which the property shall be put, the length of time the arrangement shall remain in effect, and the ultimate disposition of the property itself at the end of that time.

Therefore a trust must have a creator, or grantor, it must have property, it must have a trustee to hold and administer the property, and it must have a beneficiary for whose benefit the property is held or kept by the trustee. These elements of a trust are discussed in detail later.

The laws of the various jurisdictions provide, in differing degrees of detail, for the creation, operation, and control of trusts. A trust is, therefore, a legal entity. There is wide diversity among the different state laws, but the basic principles are much the same everywhere.

As a legal entity, a trust can, through its trustee, own and manage property, operate a business, make investments, sue or be sued, be a partner in a partnership, and so on.

But stripped of its legal trappings, a trust is essentially nothing more than an arrangement by which one party entrusts money or property to another to administer for the benefit of a beneficiary.

REASONS FOR TRUSTS AND THEIR USES

A trust is a way for a person to rid himself of property while still retaining a certain amount of control over the property and the future income from it.

There are a number of reasons why a person might want to do this. He might want to relieve himself of the job of managing the property; he might want the income from the property to be taxed to someone other than himself while still retaining some control over it; he might want to get the property out of his estate while he is living and thereby avoid some estate fees and expenses, if not the unified estate tax, on it; he might want to control the property and its use and income after his death; he might want to protect others from their own inexperience and improvidence by not giving, or leaving, the property to them outright; and others.

A trust can be established to last for a specified period of time or until a certain event occurs, such as the attaining of a certain age or the death of a beneficiary. The trust property can then be passed to others or it can be returned to the grantor. The grantor can spell out almost any terms he desires in creating a trust. As an example, a man might want to give the income from a piece of property to another for a period of time without giving up the property itself permanently. He can do this by placing the property in trust with the income to go to the other person for the desired number of years but with the property to revert to him at the end of that time.

More specifically, a trust can be used to protect a family member (or someone else) from his own inability to handle money. If there is a desire, for example, to give property to a child but the child is too young or too inexperienced to handle it wisely, it can be placed in a trust for the child's benefit. Or if a man wants to leave all or a part of his estate to his wife but fears that she might soon dissipate it if she got outright ownership of it, he can leave it in trust.

He can direct that all or any portion of the income from the property be paid to the beneficiary, he can specify at what time the property or any part of it shall be turned over to the beneficiary, he can direct the disposition of the property in case of the beneficiary's death, he can, in short, and within the bounds of public policy, exercise a tremendous amount of control over the property and its income far into the future, even long after his own death.

A trust can also be a way of relieving family members of the burdensome job of managing property. It can insure an income for a widow while still preserving the property for children. It can shift income to lower bracket taxpayers. It can help to reduce or avoid estate expenses. It can help in making detailed and intricate dispositions of property, out of the question by other means, including the providing of multiple contingent beneficiaries.

The amazing flexibility of a trust makes it a device with almost unlimited possibilities for accomplishing practically any objective a person might have in connection with the disposition of his property, either while he is still living or after his death.

Here, in outline form, are a few type situations where only a trust can do the job.* They will suggest countless other situations.

---

* **Federal Tax Guide, Estate and Gift Tax Volume, 1976,** published by Prentice-Hall, Inc.

1. Brown expects to die leaving in the neighborhood of $100,000 net. He will probably be survived by his wife and two children. The children, he feels, will be able to provide for themselves. But his wife lacks the experience and capacity to handle money and to invest it wisely. By a trust Brown can make certain, short of general economic collapse, that his widow will never be in want. By giving his trustee discretion on using principal besides income, he can gear the widow's income to her actual needs. He does not have to restrict her to fixed amounts, ample in some years, inadequate in others.

2. White expects to leave about $120,000, and a wife and a child. He wants to provide for his widow, but he also wants to save taxes. He can accomplish his purpose by two trusts. The widow will get the income from both trusts. When she dies, the principal of one trust will pass under her will. The principal of the other trust will go directly to or for the benefit of the child.

3. Green is a wealthy man, but most of his capital is tied up in real estate and stock in closely held corporations. He fears there may be no ready market for either when he dies. The death taxes will have to be paid, and that may mean sacrifice sales of his frozen assets. By means of a personal life insurance trust, he can create a cash fund to pay taxes and expenses, and avoid disastrous forced sales.

4. Black thinks a trust may be the best way to solve his estate plans, but he is not sure. Furthermore, he does not want to decide at the moment what property he will put into the trust. He can make a trial run by setting up a revocable trust. He can observe how it works, and then make whatever changes appear necessary.

5. Gray expects to leave a large, involved estate. He expects that a son and two married daughters will survive him. His wife is dead. His son has had little or no experience in financial matters. He wants to protect his property and at the same time give the boy practice in handling large sums of money. He can do this by creating a trust with two co-trustees. One will be the son. The other will be an institution or individual of proven ability, under whose guidance the son may learn.

Many other uses of trusts will be pointed out in the descriptions of various kinds of trusts in Chapter 2.

OTHER FIDUCIARY RELATIONSHIPS

Trusts may be distinguished from similar relationships in which fiduciary duties and obligations are found but which lack one or more of the essential characteristics of a trust. Some examples follow.

An agency is similar to a trust, but an agent may or may not hold title to property on behalf of his principal; he is always subject to the control of his principal; and his powers are generally less broad than those of a trustee.

A bailment differs from a trust in that it can only exist with regard to chattel property, not real property; the bailee has no title to the property, only the right of possession; and income from the property belongs to the bailor.

Other fiduciary relationships would be executors of estates, who generally have broader powers than trustees; guardianships, in which property need not be involved; receiverships; corporate directorships; and others.

EXPRESS OR IMPLIED TRUSTS

Trusts are classified according to the manner of their creation. Where created by some manifestation by the grantor, they are called "express trusts." The person having the power to create it expresses an intent to create that relationship which the law recognizes as a trust. This may be by words or by conduct or by both.

The word "trust" need not be used, nor is it necessary that the intention be known to the beneficiaries or others. But it is necessary that the grantor's intent be expressed at a time when he *owns* the property with which he intends to create the trust, and the grantor must intend for the trust to take effect immediately, not at some future time (except in the case of a testamentary trust). A written trust instrument is not always even necessary, though it is desirable, of course, for many reasons.

When a trust is based on an inferred or presumed intent of the grantor rather than on his express intent it is known as a "resulting trust." It is still a trust based on the owner's intent and does not arise just by operation of law. It might also arise as a remedy given the grantor, or those claiming under him, where a trust fails, or where the trust objectives are accomplished without exhausting the trust property and no alternative disposition has been specified.

When called into existence by court action in order to correct some injustice, without regard to the intent of the parties, a trust is called a "constructive trust." It is not really a trust at all but is a relationship with respect to property which is called a "trust" in order to impose fiduciary obligations on the person holding title to the property, as when a person has acquired it in such a way as to be under an equitable duty to convey it to another because he acquired it by fraud, duress, or mistake. Or, if an express trust has terminated or failed for some reason and it would be inequitable for the trustee to keep the property outright, a constructive trust is inferred by law.

An express trust is, of course, by far the most common kind, and the discussion throughout this book will be concerned only with this kind of trust. Trusts are also classified in other ways, such as private or charitable, active or passive, but these are discussed in the following chapter.

THE TRUST GRANTOR

Although it is possible for a trust to come into being without any real expression of trust intent (resulting and constructive trusts), an express trust can be created only by a person, known as the grantor of the trust. This person may also be called a trustor, settlor, testator, or feoffor.

Generally, any person who owns property, or any interest in property, may create a trust with regard to the property. However, if he attempts to make a trust while living, he must have the capacity to make conveyances of property; if he attempts to create a testamentary trust by his will, he must have the capacity to be a testator. Depending on local law, certain legal disabilities, such as not being of age, not being mentally competent, and others, may make his act void or voidable.

To create a trust, a grantor must first own property, and he must convey this property to a trustee (except that it is possible for a grantor to declare himself trustee, in which case no conveyance is necessary). He then has no rights or interest in the property other than ones he may have reserved for himself, such as the right to revoke the trust or to terminate it. Otherwise, complete title is vested in the trustee subject to the equitable ownership of the beneficiaries.

Whatever rights are reserved by the grantor may be transferred by him to another, and they can be reached by his creditors. (And creditors can always reach the trust property if it is shown that the trust was created in fraud of creditors.)

A person should be extremely well advised before conveying property in trust. His objectives should be clear, and he should be certain that the trust he creates will accomplish those objectives. For example, if his purpose is to reduce income taxes by passing income to others, he should be careful not to retain such powers as to cause the trust to be held a "grantor trust" with the income being taxed to him. A trust may be effective for some purposes while being ineffective for others. This is discussed in later sections.

THE TRUST PROPERTY

The only element which is absolutely essential in every kind of trust is a trust *res,* or property. Courts will supply a trustee, in certain cases they will even select beneficiaries, but in no case will they furnish the trust property. This emphasizes the fact that a trust is primarily a relationship with respect to *property.*

Every kind of valuable property capable of being transferred can be the subject matter of a trust. It can be real or personal, legal or equitable, tangible or intangible. Undivided interests and contingent interests can become the corpus of a trust, so long as they are transferable.

The *res* must be an existing interest in existing property; an interest which has not yet come into existence cannot be held in trust.

The property must be capable of being conveyed, because a trust can usually be created only by some kind of conveyance, and it must actually be conveyed, as by deed, to the trustee.

And the property must be identifiable by its nature and actually identified or described with such certainty that it can be ascertained from the existing facts. It may consist of a fractional, undivided interest in specific goods.

The grantor should select the trust property with care. He should first decide that he can safely afford to dispose of the property and, next, that the particular property is the kind that will accomplish his objectives for the trust—that it is income-producing property or growth property, property difficult to manage or easy to manage, and the like, whatever kind is best suited for the specific purposes.

THE TRUSTEE

Any natural person capable of taking title to property can receive a conveyance as trustee. Whether he can function in that capacity is another question. Although qualified to take title, some individuals may have to be replaced because they are incapable of functioning as trustee by reason of infancy or physical or mental disability.

A person nominated as trustee by the grantor of the trust usually has the privilege of accepting or declining the nomination. If the named trustee declines, or if he cannot qualify, or if the grantor failed to name a trustee, the court will appoint a trustee.

The court or the trust instrument may require a trustee to post a bond for the faithful performance of his duties.

Upon confirmation of his nomination by the court, the trustee takes title to the trust property and may proceed with the duties of administering the trust. But, again, this title is a legal title only and the trustee has no beneficial ownership of the property.

After having accepted his appointment, a trustee cannot simply resign; he must obtain an order from the court relieving him of his duties.

The court also has the power to remove a trustee if, for any reason, it appears to be in the best interests of the beneficiaries. And, of course, the death of the trustee will terminate his tenure in the position, in which case the court will direct the transfer of title in the trust property to a successor trustee.

The grantor has the privilege of naming two or more persons as cotrustees; he may name an alternate trustee to serve in case the first individual named refuses or fails to qualify; and he may name a successor trustee to serve if that becomes necessary.

Corporations, as well as individuals, can serve as trustees provided their charters permit this. Many banks and trust companies are, therefore, named as trustees. A corporation may also be named as cotrustee, alternate trustee, or successor trustee.

A grantor should select his trustee with great care and pick someone who is reliable and knowledgeable enough to do the job required in the particular case. Often, a family member might be chosen, but if the trust is larger than average or if more than average difficulty is expected in the administration, someone with more experience might be needed. Perhaps a business partner or some other business associate would be a good trustee. Or a lawyer might be selected—most lawyers are extremely knowledgeable and competent in trust administration. Or perhaps the grantor's accountant, who is familiar with his business and tax situation and who might be familiar with many phases of trust administration and taxation, would be good.

But many grantors making this decision prefer to name a trust company instead of an individual. Trust companies offer the advantages of long experience, permanence (desirable since trusts generally last for a long time), and objectivity, which may appeal to the grantor. They are willing to accept the nomination as trustee for any trust, no matter how large or small, and they will do a reliable job. The only possible disadvantages are that a trust company might not be able to take the personal interest in the trust that some individual might take and that it will have to be compensated as trustee, which a family member or some other person might not choose to be.

A testator, in writing a will which contains a testamentary trust, should name both an executor and a trustee. The two can be the same, but if so it should be remembered that the two *offices* are not the same and there is no relation of the acts in one capacity with those in the other.

A more detailed discussion of the duties and responsibilities of a trustee in administering a trust is given in Chapter 3.

BENEFICIARIES OF THE TRUST

In order to create a valid express trust the grantor must designate or provide a means for ascertaining one or more beneficiaries (also known as *cestuis que trust*) who can enforce the duties owed by the trustee and the rights created in the trust property. The trust will fail if there is no beneficiary named, or if the description of the named beneficiary is too vague and indefinite. (This, however, is not always true in the case of a charitable trust.)

There are two kinds of beneficiaries. One is the "income beneficiary," who receives the income from the trust property while the trust is in effect. The other is known as a "remainderman" (or corpus beneficiary), and he succeeds to the property itself upon the expiration of the trust term or the termination of the trust. The two may or may not be the same, and it is possible for the grantor himself to be either one or both of these.

It is extremely important for accounting and tax purposes, as will be seen later, that there be a definite distinction between the income beneficiaries and the corpus beneficiaries, or remaindermen.

Any person, or other entity, capable of holding title to property may be the beneficiary of a trust, and this includes minors and incompetents.

The important thing is that the beneficiaries be sufficiently identified. Specific identification is not necessary at the time the trust is created if the trust instrument gives a description by which the beneficiaries can be identified later. For example, a conveyance to A in trust for his life, the remainder to A's children, is valid, even if A had no children at the time the trust was created.

There can be more than one income beneficiary and there can be more than one remainderman, and there is no requirement that each be treated alike. The grantor has complete freedom in designating any portion of the income, or any portion of the remainder, to each different beneficiary. He may even grant the trustee the power to allocate or apportion the benefits among members of a designated group.

Very often the beneficiaries are not specifically named but are designated as members of a class of persons, and this is valid provided the class is described with sufficient certainty. The terms, "children," "brothers and sisters," "nephews and nieces," describe a sufficiently definite class. The term, "family," has also been held to be definite enough and generally means one's wife, children, and others living with him in a family relationship. But the term, "friends," for example, is generally held to be too vague.

A corporation can be a beneficiary, and partnerships and associations are generally considered eligible to be beneficiaries. Also eligible would be a designated class or group, such as "the members of my literary club."

In a trust with a valid beneficiary, the beneficiary is recognized as being the equitable owner of the trust property, and he has personal rights against the trustee to have the trust carried out properly. His interest may be for a certain number of years, for his lifetime, or an absolute interest. It may be contingent or vested, subject to conditions, and so on. And in some cases it may be transferrable, as discussed in a later section.

VALID AND ILLEGAL TRUSTS

A trust can be created for any lawful purpose. Usually, the grantor's objective is to promote or secure the welfare of some individual, such as his wife or a child; this, of course, is certainly a valid trust purpose. But if the terms of a trust are illegal or its objectives, probable effects, or the manner of its creation are forbidden by law or public policy it can be invalid.

Illegal trusts include those to discourage marriage, to encourage divorce, to promote criminality or other illegal or unsocial conduct, or to reward a person for committing an immoral act, and others.

One of the most frequently encountered illegal trust purposes is where a grantor makes a trust conveyance which thereby renders him insolvent, or a conveyance made with actual intent to hinder, delay, or defraud his creditors. This is an illegal, fraudulent conveyance and subject to invalidation under state or federal law. In such cases, an injured creditor can set the trust aside, at least to the extent necessary to satisfy his claim. However, if the creditors do not attack the trust the beneficiaries can enforce it.

If some particular clause of a trust is void as being against public policy and if this clause is incidental or subsidiary, it may be invalidated and the rest of the trust may still be enforced.

PERPETUAL TRUSTS

Another kind of trust which may be illegal is one created to last perpetually, or in which the beneficiary's interests do not vest in him for an unduly long period.

The rule governing this, commonly called the Rule against Perpetuities, has been stated as follows, "No interest is good unless it must vest, if at all, not later than twenty-one years after some life in being at the creation of the interest." (A *charitable* trust, however, may be created to continue perpetually.) This rule has to do only with the period within which contingent property rights must vest in interest, not in possession. It is in effect in nearly all states. But most states hold such trusts invalid only to the extent they may last longer than the permissible period; only the excessive duration is voided.

If the grantor provides that the trust is to begin if a named event occurs, and if the happening of this event is uncertain, then the legal interest of the trustee and the equitable interest of the beneficiaries are contingent at the time the instrument goes into effect. Thus, according to several cases, trusts to begin if and when an orchestra is established in a certain city, if and when a gravel pit is worked out, or if and when a mortgage is paid off out of rents, violate the rule and are void.

TRANSFER OF BENEFICIARY'S INTEREST

Since the beneficiary is the equitable owner of the trust property, he has the power to transfer his interest in it in the same way he could transfer any other property he owns. Unless there is a provision in the trust instrument preventing it, he can not only transfer his interest but he can assign it, pledge it, encumber it, or even transfer it in trust for another; and if the interest is not terminated by his death it will pass, upon his death, by his will or by intestacy law.

Although no written instrument is required in such a transfer of personal property, a transfer of real property does require one.

No consideration is necessary; the transfer can be a gift, and it can be irrevocable. Nor is it necessary to give notice to the trustee.

The power of a beneficiary to transfer his interest emphasizes again the fact that he is the equitable *owner* of his interest in the trust property. But, of course, he can transfer only those rights as were given to him by the trust, such as the right to the trust income, the right to the property itself, and so on.

CREATION OF LIVING TRUSTS

A living trust, also known as an *inter-vivos trust,* is one created by a person during his lifetime, to take effect at once, as opposed to a trust provided for in his will, to take effect at his death (a testamentary trust).

There must be an immediate present transfer of the trust property to the trustee, unless the grantor himself is trustee. A promise to transfer property in the future does not create a living trust. If the trust property is personal property, it must be physically delivered to the trustee; if it is real property the grantor must make an effective conveyance of title, usually by deed. If the grantor himself is the trustee, the delivery is considered effective if he actually segregates the trust property from his other property with the intent that it be trust property.

Notice to the trustee of the intent to form a trust is not necessary (though he must be notified when the trust is created); nor is such notice to the beneficiary necessary. However, the trustee does have the right to disclaim the position, and a beneficiary may also reject whatever rights or obligations the trust gives him (though he must accept or reject the whole trust, not just parts of it).

Consideration is not necessary in the formation of a trust; in fact, most transfers to trusts are gifts.

As for the form of instrument required in the creation of a trust, great latitude is permitted. If the trust consists of personal property only, no written instrument at all is required in most states; an oral trust will suffice, though one in writing spelling out the provisions in detail is certainly preferable. But trusts of real estate must be evidenced by some writing signed by the grantor. This may be a simple memorandum, but it must be complete and contain the essential terms of the trust.

But to clearly express the grantor's intentions and to save future trouble and misunderstandings, a carefully drawn trust instrument should be prepared, and this instrument should clearly designate the trust property, it should name a trustee (and probably an alternate and successor trustee), it should clearly designate the beneficiary or beneficiaries and define the exact interest of each in the income from the property or in the property itself, and it should specify the term of the trust or the event which will cause the termination of the trust.

CREATION OF TESTAMENTARY TRUSTS

A testamentary trust is one provided for in a person's will, and it must contain the essential trust elements, such as the designation of the trust property, the beneficiaries, the trustee, and the trust purposes. The will must, of course, be a valid will or the trust will not be valid.

An inter-vivos trust will be held to be testamentary if it depends on the decedent's will, as, for example, when no real interest passes during the grantor's lifetime. Or, if the beneficiaries can be ascertained only by some future testamentary act it will be, in effect, a testamentary trust. The same is true if the trust property is to be designated by the grantor's will, because there is no *present* trust transfer. And, for estate tax purposes, it will be held to be testamentary if the grantor retained any major degree of control over the trust or its administration or enjoyment.

Testamentary trusts are extremely common. A decedent can leave his property in only two ways, either outright or in trust, and there are frequently compelling reasons for not leaving it outright. As mentioned earlier, the testator might want it to go to some minor who is incapable of handling it, or he might want to leave it to his widow but fear that she would dissipate it, or he might want the income to go to certain beneficiaries for a period of time with the property itself going to others later. These and many other situations make a testamentary trust the ideal way to accomplish certain objectives.

Either all or only a specified portion of the decedent's property can be designated as trust property. Or a percentage of the residue, for example, can be so designated. More than one trust can be provided for, each having a different objective, and so on. There is much flexibility, and a testator can provide for a trust, or trusts, in his will which will satisfy any desire he might have in connection with any part of his estate or with any of his different beneficiaries.

But it is very important for a testator to first have clearly in mind exactly what he wants to accomplish and then to be sure that the trust provisions in his will are drafted in such a way as to meet all the requirements of a testamentary trust and that they will govern according to his wishes after his death.

TRANSFERS IN TRUST AS GIFTS

Most inter-vivos trusts are created by a *gift* of property to the trust. There is seldom any consideration involved. Testamentary trusts, however, do not fall into the category of gifts but are, rather, legacies of property to a trust.

An inter-vivos transfer in trust is therefore, a gift and it is usually subject to the gift tax. It must, however, constitute a complete transfer; incomplete transfers are not taxed as gifts. A trust which is revocable by the grantor is regarded as an incomplete transfer, but if the grantor later surrenders such a power the gift is taxable. And certain other powers retained by the grantor, such as the power to modify the trust, to change the beneficiary, to alter the beneficiary's interest, and the like, will render the transfer incomplete for gift tax purposes. A transfer is not subject to the gift tax until there is cessation of the grantor's dominion and control.

The gift tax consequences should be considered by a person contemplating the creation of a trust. The gift tax on a large transfer might be so great that a person would decide he could not afford to make the transfer; and he might be reluctant to start using up his unified gift and estate tax credit. But this is not always the case, because the gift tax marital deduction under the 1976 law and the $3,000 per donee annual exclusions make it possible to make a rather large gift and still pay little or no gift tax on the transfer.

TERMINATION OF A TRUST

The terms of the trust instrument generally govern the time for termination of a trust. A specific period of time may have been established for the trust to continue, or the happening of a certain event may have been designated to control the time of termination. If so, these usually govern.

But if the grantor reserved the right to terminate the trust he may do so at his pleasure. (And if he has this power he is usually deemed also to have the power to modify the trust.) In this connection, the grantor must choose between making his trust revocable and probably subjecting himself to income taxes, or making it irrevocable and subjecting himself to gift taxes.

As for the trustee, he has no power to terminate the trust unless it was specifically given to him by the trust instrument. Such a power is often given the trustee, and it may even be a discretionary power which he may exercise based on his best judgment.

The beneficiaries have a very limited power to terminate a trust. They can do so only if all of them, being legally competent, join in a suit to terminate the trust and it appears that termination will not defeat the grantor's material purpose in creating the trust.

But a court may authorize termination when it appears that continuance of the trust would jeopardize the grantor's original purpose.

Finally, when the trust property ceases to exist, as when it has all been distributed, used up, or lost, the trust will terminate by operation of law.

At the termination of the trust, the trustee is normally under a duty to deliver the remaining property to the proper beneficiaries. This is done by simply delivering personal property to the remainderman or by making a legal conveyance in the case of real property. When the trust is to end at a fixed date, as, for example, at the death of a named person, the powers of the trustee which are necessary for settlement and distribution continue for a period needed to accomplish those objectives.

2

THE KINDS OF TRUSTS

All trusts contain the same basic trust elements, but trusts can be classified in many, many different ways, based on the manner of, or reason for, their creation and the purposes, or objectives, of the particular trust.

The two broadest classifications, express or implied trusts and inter-vivos or testamentary trusts, were discussed in the preceding chapter, but three additional general classifications are given here. This is followed by descriptions of a number of specific kinds of trusts, each usually designed with some specific purpose in mind and most often taking its name (or nick-name) from that purpose.

There can be much overlapping between one kind of trust and another. Many trusts will be designed to accomplish several different objectives at the same time and may, therefore, contain features from several of the different kinds of trusts discussed in this chapter.

CHARITABLE OR PRIVATE TRUSTS

A charitable trust is one that is established for the public benefit, either for the entire public or for some particular class of persons, indefinite in number, who constitute a part of the public. Most often of

33

course, the trust beneficiary is some established charitable organization through which members of the public are reached with the ultimate benefits, but it is not at all necessary that an organization be so named; the trustee himself can be the one who determines and directs the distribution of the benefits, within the limitations of the trust instrument.

All other trusts are known as private trusts; that is, they have as their beneficiaries certain individuals rather than the public and have no charitable purpose as the term is generally used.

Private trusts are probably used much more often than charitable trusts, but charitable trusts are common enough to warrant a section later in this chapter giving a summary of their characteristics as a specific kind of trust.

ACTIVE OR PASSIVE TRUSTS

The classification of trusts as active or passive is of little practical importance under present law, because in most jurisdictions a passive trust is void. But, historically, an active trust was one in which the trustee had *any* specific duties in the management or administration of the trust property, as contrasted with one in which he had no real duties but simply held the legal title to the property for someone else. A trust, however, will generally be considered active if the trustee has *any* power or duty requiring discretion on his part.

REVOCABLE OR IRREVOCABLE TRUSTS

The grantor of a trust can retain for himself the power to terminate the trust, or to alter or amend it. This power to revoke the trust will, of course, classify the trust as a revocable one. If no such powers are retained and if the grantor, by the terms he established in the trust instrument, is completely unable to terminate or alter the provisions, the trust is known as an irrevocable trust.

A person unwilling to give up total or permanent control of the trust property can still get the benefits of a trust by using a revocable trust. There are many advantages of revocable trusts, some of which are as follows:*

1. The revocable trust takes the place of a will for the trust property. It controls unless it is revoked. It gives the settlor far more privacy than a will.

* Federal Tax Guide, Estate and Gift Tax Volume, 1976, published by Prentice-Hall, Inc.

2. It can be amended or altered, because the power to revoke includes the lesser powers.

3. If the situation changes, beneficiaries or benefits can be changed.

4. The trustee's powers can be changed, enlarged or limited, if experience makes it desirable.

5. The items in the trust corpus can be changed. The grantor can take investments out and put others in, at will.

6. He can put in or take out spendthrift and similar provisions, according to how the beneficiaries demonstrate their ability to handle money. There need be no guesswork here.

7. He can see how much income the trust actually earns. Then he can permit a more liberal use of corpus if needed.

8. He can change the trustee, or add co-trustees.

9. He can always make the trust irrevocable, by releasing the power to revoke. He might want to do this to protect the trust property against creditors if he were about to venture his outside capital in some uncertain enterprise.

10. This is really the key to the whole thing. The grantor of the trust can *watch it work*. He can change the instrument, as seen above, and he can also clarify any provision that raises doubts.

But there are distinct disadvantages too. For income tax purposes, if a trust is revocable it is known as a "grantor trust" (discussed in more detail later) and the trust income will be taxed to the grantor just as if the trust had not been set up. So if the objective of the trust is to shift taxable income away from the grantor and to someone else, the trust generally must be an irrevocable one. Certain other retained powers, discussed later, may also render the trust invalid for tax purposes.

It can readily be seen that deciding whether to make a trust revocable or irrevocable is one of the most important decisions facing a person contemplating the use of a trust. The purposes of the trust must be clearly decided upon, and this as well as other factors must govern the final decision. The importance of this election cannot be overemphasized; a mistake at this point can destroy the entire future of the trust and leave the grantor with only expense and trouble instead of the expected advantages.

GRANTOR TRUSTS

Although a trust might be a valid one in every way, it might still not be recognized for income tax purposes. This is true, as indicated above, when the grantor has retained such powers as to be considered, under the Internal Revenue Code, as the owner of the trust. (And this may also be true if the power is held not by the grantor himself but by some other person whose actions may be attributable to the grantor.) Such trusts are commonly called "grantor trusts," and the income from these trusts will be taxed to the grantor.

The Code goes into great detail in spelling out just what conditions will cause a trust to be considered as owned by the grantor, but the more important of these provisions are summarized in the following paragraphs.

A grantor is taxed on trust income from property in which he retains a reversionary interest (the possibility of it coming back to him) in the corpus or income, if the reversionary interest may take effect within ten years after the transfer of the property to the trust.

He is taxed on the trust income if he has the power to dispose of the trust property or income without the consent of any party whose interests are adverse to his. (But there are several exceptions to this general rule.)

A trust is also a grantor trust if the grantor has administrative control of the trust which may be exercised primarily for his own benefit instead of that of the beneficiaries, such as to borrow from the trust without adequate interest or security, to direct the voting of stock owned by the trust, to reacquire the trust property by substituting other property of an equivalent value, and others.

The reserved power to revoke or alter the trust will cause the trust to be a grantor trust. However, this is not true if the grantor can revoke it only with the consent of an adverse party. And, if he cannot exercise the power to revoke the trust until ten years after the inception of the trust, he is not taxed on the income during that time; he will be taxed on the income after that time, unless he gives up the power to revoke the trust.

The grantor is taxed on any trust income that is or may be, in his discretion, distributed to him, held or accumulated for him, or applied to the payment of premiums on his life insurance; and, as to income from property placed in trust after October 9, 1969, this provision includes the grantor's wife also. Also, he is taxed on income that is used to satisfy his (or his wife's) legal obligation to support someone.

A testamentary trust is never a grantor trust because it does not come into being until after the death of the testator, from which time, of course, he can have no powers.

This brief discussion of grantor trusts is perhaps an oversimplification of a very complex subject which is covered in much detail in the income tax and estate tax law and regulations, to which the reader should refer for much more specific information if necessary in any particular case.

SHORT-TERM TRUSTS

A trust established for a certain period of time, with the property to revert to the grantor at the end of that time, would seem to be a grantor trust. However, the income tax law provides for an exception in certain cases. If the trust term is for at least ten years and a day, this is a so-called "short-term" trust, also commonly known as a "Clifford" trust, and the income will be taxed to the trust or the beneficiary, not to the grantor. Or, if the trust income is payable to a beneficiary for life, with a reversion in the grantor, the grantor is not taxed on the income even if the life expectancy of the beneficiary is less than ten years.

However, if property is added to the trust during the ten (or more) year term without any provision for extending the term of the trust so that the new property will be in trust for more than ten years, the grantor is taxable on the income from the property involved in the second transfer.

Short-term trusts provide an advantage over other kinds of trusts in that they permit the return of the trust principal to the grantor after he has passed along the income tax burden to someone else for a stated period. This technique permits the high-bracket income earner to transfer away income-producing property and provide for members of his family.

Some uses to which short-term trusts can be put are to take care of a relative whom the grantor has no legal obligation to support and thereby divert taxable income to a lower-bracket taxpayer; to accumulate savings for children; to carry insurance on the life of certain family members (other than the owner of the property in trust); to accumulate funds to be available as liquid estate assets; and so on.

Again, a short-term trust must last more than ten years or for the life of the income beneficiary. The trust can be for ten years and a day or it can extend far beyond ten years. The economics of each situation should dictate. For example, a trust timed to end after the grantor has retired will return the income to him at a time when his high income sources may have dried up.

Pitfalls of grantor control must be avoided. A trust term in excess of ten years will not insulate the grantor from tax if he keeps control (enforceable within the ten-year period) of the beneficial enjoyment or retains any of the other marks of ownership discussed above.

A transfer to a short-term trust is a gift, subject to the gift tax. The taxable value of the gift is measured by the actuarial value of the property at the date of the gift (about 44 percent of the principal for a ten-year trust), determined from actuarial tables in the regulations.

MARITAL DEDUCTION TRUSTS

One of the basic and most important tools in estate planning is the marital deduction, and this very often takes the form of a trust.

A person's gross estate at his death (less the deductions for debts, administrative expenses, taxes, and losses) may be reduced by the amount of any of his property he leaves to his spouse, up to a maximum deduction of 50 percent of that gross figure (as reduced), or $250,000, whichever is greater, in arriving at the taxable estate figure. This is the marital deduction.

This is a tremendous tax-saving device, and, almost invariably, a testator will endeavor to make the best possible use of it.

The property must be left, however, in such a way as to qualify as marital deduction property, and the estate tax law has a very great deal to say about the specific qualifications for such property. But, very briefly, it boils down to the requirement that the property must be left in such a way that the survivor has almost complete ownership or control of it and that it, or the part remaining at the survivor's death, will be taxed in that estate. If it is left in such a way that the spouse's interest in it will, or may, terminate or fail, it will not qualify; this is the "terminable interest rule."

A complete discussion of the very important marital deduction is beyond the scope of this book, but, again briefly, it is obvious that property will qualify for the marital deduction if it is left to the surviving spouse outright. But what about property left in trust? It will also qualify if the following conditions are met:

The surviving spouse must be entitled to all the income from the entire interest or the income from a specific portion, for life; the income must be payable at least annually or at more frequent intervals; the surviving spouse must have the power to appoint the entire property or the specific portion to herself or her estate; the power must be exercisable by the survivor alone, and in all events, whether by will, or during life; the property interest must not be subject to the power in any other person to appoint to someone other than the surviving spouse. If these conditions are met, the survivor's interest is not "terminable."

Therefore, testamentary trusts are very commonly used for the marital deduction property left to the survivor, and the principal reason is, of course, that the testator might fear that his spouse would be so inexperienced in money matters, or so extravagant, or gullible, that she would soon spend or lose her inheritance and suffer because of it. A trust is the ideal way to protect the survivor from herself in such cases, and a trust consisting of the property qualifying for the marital deduction is what is known as a "marital deduction trust."

The testator can provide for the income only to go to his spouse (along with her power to appoint the property), if he thinks that will be sufficient, or for some of the principal to be used, or for the trustee to have discretion in the use of the principal, and so on. There is much flexibility possible within the tax requirements.

The entire estate, not just the marital deduction portion, might be left in trust to the survivor. Or, the testator might choose to leave his spouse just enough to qualify for the marital deduction, and leave the second half to others. This is common in estate planning because it means that this second portion of the property will by-pass the survivor's estate and save a second, unnecessary tax on it. This second half may also be left either outright or in trust, as, for example, a trust for children, and the income from that trust might also go to the survivor for her life-time. If there is a second trust, it is usually called a "non-marital deduction trust," and when this arrangement is used the trusts are commonly referred to as A and B trusts, the A trust meaning the marital deduction trust and the B trust meaning the non-marital deduction trust.

A slightly different form of marital deduction trust is one known as an "estate trust," in which the trust property passes only to the surviving spouse's estate upon her death. The survivor can direct, in her will, what will happen to it when she dies. The income may be paid to the spouse for life or may be accumulated with the corpus plus accumulated income going to the spouse's estate. This is not a terminable interest because no one other than the surviving spouse or her estate ever has any interest in the property. If the income from the property is made payable to another individual for life or for a term of years, with the remainder absolutely to the surviving spouse or her estate, the marital deduction is based on the present value (at the time of the testator's death) of the remainder. An estate trust is a highly recommended form of marital deduction trust, provided that there is no question of the income being ample for the survivor's needs; but even if there is such a question, it can be answered by simply giving the trustee the power to distribute principal to the survivor.

POWER OF APPOINTMENT TRUSTS

A power of appointment is a right to designate, by will or by deed, the persons who are to receive certain property placed in trust. Such a power is usually held by someone who has the income from the property for life - a life tenant. But it is possible, of course, for one person to have the life income and another person to have the right to designate who shall receive the property after the death of the life tenant.

Any trust (usually but not necessarily testamentary) granting such a power to someone can be called a "power of appointment trust."

A power to appoint is frequently granted to the surviving spouse; this was mentioned earlier as one of the ways to qualify a trust for the marital deduction. But it is possible for someone other than the survivor to have a power of appointment, in a non-marital deduction trust.

There is some tax danger to the holder of a power of appointment. If he has the power to vest corpus or income in himself he will find that the income of the trust is taxable to him. In addition, if he formerly had such a power but released it, retaining any of the powers that would cause trust income to be taxable to a grantor, he will also be taxed as if he were a grantor.

And if this holder has a "general" power of appointment (the right to dispose of the property to himself, his estate, his creditors, or the creditors of his estate), the property would be a part of his taxable estate at this death.

The donee of a power of appointment does not always have the opportunity beforehand of accepting or refusing the power. If one is granted to him, he may prefer not to have it on account of the potential estate tax liability due to the property being in his estate. In this case, he may disclaim or renounce the power, provided he does so within a reasonable period after having learned of its existence. The donee may also escape estate tax liability by releasing or exercising the power, provided he reserves no rights such as would cause a transfer of his own property during his lifetime to be included in his estate. Or, to avoid tax in the holder's estate, the power should be drawn in such a way that it cannot be exercised for the benefit of himself, his estate, or his creditors.

SPRINKLING TRUSTS

In the case of any trust, either inter-vivos or testamentary, other than a marital deduction trust, trustees may be given the discretion to distribute income as they may determine among a group or class of beneficiaries. Such a "sprinkling trust" can be very useful in equalizing the financial situations of the beneficiaries and can also produce substantial income tax savings by permitting the trustee to distribute disproportionate amounts of income to lower-bracket recipients. This sprinkling principle may also be extended to discretionary powers to invade corpus.

Sprinkling trusts have great flexibility. For example, where the testator has more than one child, he may provide separate trusts for each child and his or her descendents with sprinkling powers so that income may be divided among members of that child's family. The tax-saving potential in such an arrangement is obvious. And recipients of the "sprinkled" income can even include other trusts. The more income beneficiaries there are, each being a separate taxable entity, the greater the income tax saving.

SKIP-A-GENERATION TRUSTS

A "skip-a-generation trust" is also a popular tax saving device. It is usually testamentary, but its principles can also be used in living trusts.

If a testator's children themselves have substantial estates, either through prior inheritance (for example, from their grandparents) or of their own accumulation, the testator might decide that it would be unwise to leave his property to them, as it would increase their taxable income during their lifetimes and would increase their already large estates upon their deaths. Why not skip that generation and leave the property to the childrens' children? They are the ones who would likely get it later anyway, and it by-passes the childrens' large estates. Not only is one estate tax avoided but a second estate tax is postponed, probably far into the future, until the grandchildren die.

If this plan is decided upon, the property can be left outright to the grandchildren, but leaving it in a trust, or trusts, might be much better; and it might be necessary if the grandchildren are too young to handle the property. If the testator has more than one child, a separate trust could be provided for each child's children. And each child, himself, could be named the trustee for that trust; this is commonly done.

If the testator has more grandchildren than children—often the case— it can be seen that a skip-a-generation trust has some of the elements and advantages of a sprinkling trust.

A slight variation in a skip-a-generation trust would be to leave the property in trust with the child to get the income from it for his lifetime and with the principal going to his children at his death. The property, again, by-passes the child's estate (except for the 1976 law, below). The tax-saving potential of a skip-a-generation trust is great.

But some of the advantages of this kind of trust were lessened by the Tax Reform Act of 1976, which imposed a new tax on certain generation-skipping transfers. A generation-skipping transfer is defined as either a "taxable termination" of a beneficiary's interest or a "taxable distribution" to a beneficiary of a generation-skipping trust, and a generation-skipping trust is one with *two or more* generations of beneficiaries (income or corpus) belonging to a generation younger than the grantor.

A taxable event occurs when the interest of a younger generation beneficiary (child, for example) who is older than any other younger generation beneficiary (grandchild) comes to an end, or when a distribution is made to a younger generation beneficiary (such as a grandchild) and there is another younger generation beneficiary (a child, for example) who belongs to an older generation than the recipient.

The tax imposed is substantially equivalent to the estate or gift tax that would have been imposed if the property had been transferred outright and is the difference between the tax on the transferred property plus all other taxable transfers and the tax computed on those other transfers alone. It is paid out of the trust property.

But in spite of the present law, there are still several tax-saving possibilities. For example, a trust for the grantor's spouse for life with remainder to a grandchild would not be a generation-skipping trust because there are not *two or more* generations of beneficiaries younger than the grantor, and the grantor's child's estate would be effectively bypassed. As another possibility, if the trust gives income to a child for life, then to a grandchild for life with the remainder to a greatgrandchild, and the grandchild dies first, there is no taxable termination on his death because he never held a *present* income interest.

Further, amounts subject to estate or gift tax are not included in taxable terminations or distributions, so if a trust's income is left to a child for his life, then to a grandchild for life with a general power of appointment, there is no taxable termination on the grandchild's death because the property is subject to estate tax in his estate due to his having had the general power of appointment.

And, finally, transfers to grandchildren are not subject to the tax to the extent the total transfers do not exceed $250,000 through a transferor such as the grantor's child who is also the grandchild's parent. Thus, if the grantor has two children each of whom has children, up to $500,000 can be transferred to the grandchildren tax free.

The generation-skipping tax generally applies to transfers that occur after April 30, 1976, but it does not apply in cases of transfers under irrevocable trusts in existence on that date or for decedents dying before January 1, 1982 under a will or revocable trust in existence on and not amended after that date.

POUR-OVER TRUSTS

Since a trust affords more privacy in the disposition of a person's property than a will does, there is a trend toward the use of a living trust instead of a testamentary trust for handling property left by a decedent. A will must be probated and becomes a part of the public record; anyone can learn of its provisions, including any testamentary trusts it might contain. A trust instrument, however, does not usually have to be recorded, though it may be if desired.

A plan known as a "pour-over trust" might be considered if secrecy is wanted, as it most often is, and this plan works as follows.

When writing a will, a testator can, at or about the same time, create a living trust which provides for the eventual disposition of any property coming to it. The will, then, can simply direct that the decedent's property be given to the trust. Upon the decedent's death, this will effectively conceal from the public just what will happen to the decedent's property. The will provisions will have been carried out, the estate can be settled, and the trust will take over and operate in complete privacy.

The trust so created must be a valid one, of course. It must be funded with some property at the time it is created, but this can be anything, even, for example, $50 in cash. And, as with any trust, it can provide for either the immediate disposition of the property or for the trust to operate over a number of years into the future.

A testamentary trust can have no real advantages over this kind of arrangement.

But it must be remembered that property going to a trust is *not* property going to a surviving spouse and will not qualify for the marital deduction unless the trust contains the proper provisions to qualify it as a marital deduction trust, discussed earlier.

DISCRETIONARY TRUSTS

As indicated several times before, a grantor may give his trustee discretion as to which beneficiaries to pay the trust income to. The trustee may also be given the power to decide whether to pay out *any* of the income or to withhold it, and he may be given similar powers over the trust corpus. When a trustee has any such powers, the trust may be called a "discretionary trust."

It is very often wise for a grantor to give his trustee some discretion, in one way or another depending on the trust's objectives. No one can foresee the future well enough to be positive that the decisions he makes at present will continue to be wise ones for ten, twenty, or more years, whatever the term of the trust might be. Situations do change constantly, and so do the needs of the various beneficiaries, so why not build into the trust enough future flexibility to prevent some undesirable things from happening later? Discretionary power is particularly desirable in a testamentary trust; the grantor will be gone, so someone in a position to watch the trust work should have the power to correct any unforeseen inequities that might develop. Discretionary powers can be as limited or as broad as the grantor, or testator, might like, but anyone establishing a trust should keep in mind the wise old saying, "a dead hand should not rule too long."

A discretionary trust is not usually just that alone, but it is more in the nature of a special feature of some other kind of trust, such as a sprinkling trust, charitable trust, and others.

One interesting, occasional use of the discretionary trust feature is when the grantor leaves the income to one person but fears that person's improvidence. He then names as an alternate beneficiary someone who bears a kindly, affectionate relationship to the primary beneficiary. Then, if the primary beneficiary has creditors, the trustee with discretionary powers can pay the income to the alternate beneficiary, who might be under a moral obligation to take care of the other.

SPENDTHRIFT TRUSTS

A spendthrift trust is one in which the beneficiary is unable voluntarily or involuntarily to transfer his interest in the trust. He cannot sell or give away his right to future income or principal, and his creditors are unable to collect or attach such rights.

It is probably safe to say that a majority of modern private express trusts contain some spendthrift provisions, and this kind of trust is usually created for the purpose of providing a fund for the maintenance of a beneficiary which will be secure against his own improvidence.

Spendthrift provisions are valid in most, but not all, jurisdictions, and they may be imposed on the right to transfer either the income or the principal, or both. When held invalid, it has usually been because of the theory that a creditor should be able to reach the assets of his debtor, whether held in trust or not.

But even if creditors cannot reach the beneficiary's interest in the trust, after monies have been paid to the beneficiary they can, of course, reach that, the same as any other asset.

The owner of property cannot create a spendthrift trust for himself and thereby put his own property beyond the reach of his creditors; this would be treated as a fraudulent conveyance and the trust would be set aside.

PROTECTIVE TRUSTS

A "protective trust" is similar to a spendthrift trust, and it is often used in states which do not recognize spendthrift trusts.

It is an ordinary trust in most ways, but it contains a provision saying that if the beneficiary attempts to transfer his interest in it, the trustee has discretionary powers to pay the trust income to any or all of a group of beneficiaries which includes the primary beneficiary. The result is much the same as with a spendthrift trust because the beneficiary can be sure of receiving the trust benefits only so long as he keeps his debts paid.

SUPPORT TRUSTS

The trustee of a "support trust" has discretionary powers to use only so much of the income as might be necessary to support the beneficiary (or pay for his education, or other specific purposes) but to use the income for no other purpose.

The beneficiary cannot assign his interest in the trust because he has no interest in it other than what the trustee decides to give him, and the trustee is limited to distributions for support only; nor is there an interest which can be reached by the beneficiary's creditors.

A support trust is another kind of trust which might attain some of the objectives of a spendthrift trust in states where spendthrifts are not valid.

BLENDED TRUSTS

Another type of trust in which the limited nature of the beneficiary's interest has the same general effect on his right to sell or transfer as a spendthrift trust is the so-called "blended trust," in which the trust is for the benefit of a group and in which the interests of two or more beneficiaries are blended in such a way that no one beneficiary can claim any particular share of its benefits. No beneficiary, therefore, has an interest that he can sell or assign or which his creditors can reach. His interest is "blended" with that of every other beneficiary.

TOTTEN TRUSTS

If a person deposits some of his own money in a bank account in his own name "as trustee for" someone else, there is a question of whether or not this constitutes a real trust. This arrangement, known as a "Totten trust," has been held by most courts, though not all, to be a valid, revocable, inter-vivos trust. The presumption is that the depositor, by his actions, expressed the intent that there be a trust.

The circumstances may vary a little in different cases, but, for example, if the depositor notified the supposed beneficiary of the deposit, this has a strong tendency to prove a real trust intent, especially if he also delivered the bank book to the beneficiary; most courts would consider this to be a trust.

A Totten trust is not a gift for gift tax purposes; there is no deflection of the taxable income away from the depositor; the depositor's creditors can reach the deposit; and, since it is a revocable trust, the unrevoked balance is includible in the depositor's estate for federal estate tax purposes.

However, anything remaining in the account at the depositor's death does go to the named beneficiary, if living, so a Totten trust is sometimes referred to as "a poor man's will."

CHARITABLE TRUSTS

The law favors a charitable trust, either inter-vivos or testamentary, with many advantages not possessed by a private trust. Courts will apply liberal rules of construction in an effort to support charitable trusts. Such trusts can be perpetual in duration, as the Rule against Perpetuities does not apply to them; they enjoy immunity from some of the rules regarding reversions of vesting and suspensions of the power of transfer; their property is generally exempt from ad valorem taxation; and they receive many privileges with respect to income, estate, and gift taxation. Also, the liberal "Cy Pres" rule, under which a court can modify a trust to meet changing conditions, is applied only to charitable trusts.

A trust must involve some public benefit before it is admitted to the privileged characterization. It must, for example, be for educational purposes, for the relief of poverty, for religious purposes, for the cure of disease and promotion of health, for governmental purposes, or others. No profit-making purposes may be allowed.

The creator of an inter-vivos charitable trust gets the advantage of an income tax deduction for the contribution (subject to certain tax rules regarding reversionary interests and others). The creator of a testamentary charitable trust will get a deduction from his gross estate for estate tax purposes. But the Code specifies that the deduction will be allowed only for transfers to or for the use of:

1. The United States, any state, territory, any political subdivision thereof, or the District of Columbia, for exclusively public purposes;

2. Any corporation or association organized and operated exclusively for religious, charitable, scientific, literary, or educational purposes (including the encouragement of art and the prevention of cruelty to children or animals), if no part of the net earnings of the corporation or association inures to the benefit of any private stockholder or individual (other than as a legitimate object of such purposes), and no substantial part of its activities is carrying on propoganda, or otherwise attempting to influence legislation;

3. A trustee or trustees, or a fraternal society, order, or association operating under the lodge system, if the transferred property is to be used exclusively for religious, charitable, scientific, literary, or educational purposes (or for the prevention of cruelty to children or animals), and if no substantial part of the activities of such transferee is carrying on propaganda, or otherwise attempting to influence legislation; or

4. Any veterans' organization incorporated by Act of Congress, or of any of its departments, local chapters, or posts, no part of the net earnings of which inures to the benefit of any private shareholder or individual.

Charitable trusts are quite common in wills. The taxes on the testator's estate will not only be reduced, as a charitable bequest is a deduction from gross estate, but there are other, less tangible, benefits. Many people who have great wealth but little or no family to leave it to will provide for a charitable trust in their wills in order to continue to fulfill their charitable desires and perhaps to perpetuate their names many, many years into the future after their deaths.

But the income and estate tax rules regarding the creation and qualifications of charitable trusts are very intricate and comprehensive, and they should be studied carefully so that the requirements may be fully met if the use of such a trust is being contemplated.

CHARITABLE REMAINDER TRUSTS

A person might want to give, or leave, property to a charity, but he might feel an obligation to provide for some individual first. He can do this by creating a "charitable remainder trust," with the income to go to the individual for a period of time or for the beneficiary's lifetime with the remainder to go to charity, or to a charitable trust, later. A trust of this kind can be either inter-vivos or testamentary.

There is some difficulty in determining the amount of the charitable deduction, for estate tax purposes, with a charitable remainder trust. The tax rules are summarized as follows:

No deduction is allowed for the bequest of a charitable remainder unless the remainder interest is in a farm or personal residence or is a trust interest in an annuity trust, unitrust, or a pooled income fund.

A <u>Charitable Remainder Annuity Trust</u> is one that pays only a specific sum to at least one noncharitable income beneficiary for his life or a term of not more than twenty years and transfers the remainder interest to a charity. The income payout must be made at least once a year and cannot be less than five percent of the value of the property when it was placed in trust.

A <u>Charitable Remainder Unitrust</u> is a trust that pays only a fixed percentage (not less than 5%) of the value of the trust property determined every year. Like an annuity trust, the payment must be made at least annually to at least one noncharitable income beneficiary and the remainder is transferred to a charity. However, the will or trust instrument may provide that the unitrust pay its income to the noncharitable beneficiary even if it is less than the required percentage, but only if the will or trust instrument also provides that the deficit is to be made up from any excess of trust income over the required percentage in subsequent years.

A <u>Pooled Income Fund</u> is a trust that is made up solely of irrevocable remainder interests contributed to the charity that maintains the fund. At the time of death, the decedent also transfers a life income interest in the property for the life of one or more named living beneficiaries. The income is payable by the fund to each beneficiary and is determined by the rate of return of the fund. Income must be distributed currently or within 65 days following the close of the tax year in which the income is earned. The estate is entitled to a charitable contribution deduction for the present value of the charitable remainder interest. This value is the present fair market value of the assets transferred less the present value of the life income interest of the noncharitable beneficiaries. The present value of a contributed remainder interest is computed on the basis of tables found in Reg. Sec. 1.642 (c)-6(d) (3) for the life of one individual and at the highest rate of return in the three years preceding the year of the transfer.

The only charitable income interests that can be deducted are guaranteed annuities or bequests of a fixed percentage distributed yearly based on the property's fair market value determined annually.

The charitable remainder and income interest rules apply to estates of decedents dying after 1969. However, they do not apply to transfers under wills executed before October 10, 1969 or transfers to trusts before October 10, 1969 if, (1) the decedent dies before October 9, 1972 without republishing the will or amending the trust after October 9, 1969, (2) the decedent did not have the right to change the will or trust instrument after October 9, 1969, or (3) the will is not republished or trust instrument not amended before October 9, 1972 and the decedent did not have the mental capacity to do so after October 8, 1972. If a transition rule applies, the deduction is allowed if the remainder interest can be ascertained. A power of invasion for the benefit of the life tenant may be allowed if the remainder interest is ascertainable. However, a conditional remainder interest is not deductible when the possibility that the charity will receive any benefit is negligible.

INSURANCE TRUSTS

A life insurance policy is property and can constitute the subject matter of a trust. An "insurance trust" may be created by a person desiring to remove the proceeds of a policy on his life from his estate, and thereby avoid some estate tax at his death, but not wanting the policy to belong to any individual. He must, of course, transfer *all* incidents of ownership in the policy to the trust, but by placing the insurance in trust he can still retain some control over it. He can direct the disposition of the proceeds upon his death, for example. Again, a trust instrument has somewhat the flexibility of a will plus the advantage of assuring more privacy about the disposition of property.

An insurance trust can be created in a variety of ways. A grantor who is the insured may retain ownership of an existing policy but name as beneficiary the trustee of an existing or newly created trust. Or, he might assign all ownership rights in an existing policy to the trustee. If a policy is not in effect, the grantor-insured may purchase one, naming the trustee as owner or initial beneficiary.

When creating an insurance trust the grantor should consider whether or not he wants it to be "funded" with securities or other assets put into the trust along with the policy to provide income to pay the insurance premiums. If it is not funded, provision should be made for some other way of paying the premiums in the future.

And the grantor might also consider borrowing against the policy before placing it in trust in order to reduce or eliminate the gift tax on the transfer.

ALIMONY TRUSTS

An "alimony trust" might be created by a husband to provide payments to a divorced wife in place of ordinary alimony payments. Or, an existing trust with the husband as grantor and the wife as beneficiary could become an alimony trust upon the divorce of the couple.

Ordinarily, the income of a trust with a wife as beneficiary is taxable to the grantor-husband under Code Sections 677 (a) and (b). But special rules in Code Section 682 govern the taxation of certain trust income between spouses who are divorced or separated under a decree or written separation agreement. The effect is to tax to the wife trust income that would otherwise have been taxable to the husband because paid in satisfaction of his legal obligation. Trust income that is paid or required to be distributed to the wife, and that otherwise would be taxed to the husband, is includible in her gross income and excludible from his. The wife is treated in all respects as a true trust beneficiary. The effect of this special rule is, of course, to tax the trust income in the same way that ordinary alimony would be taxed—taxable to the recipient and deductible by the payor.

Also under the special rules, if any portion of the trust income is specifically earmarked for the support of the grantor's minor children, such income is taxable to him, not the wife. But the language of the decree or other instrument must clearly reflect the grantor's intention; otherwise the wife may be taxed on the entire income. If the agreement expresses the amount to go to the children as a fixed sum rather than as a percentage, and the trust fails to generate enough income, then income is first applied to the satisfaction of the grantor's obligation to support the children and the reduction of the wife's share of income to that extent reduces the amount excludible by the grantor.

MASSACHUSETTS TRUSTS

A "Massachusetts trust" is a little-used form of organization for carrying on a joint venture or business operation. It is sometimes called a "business trust" or a "common-law trust." Its assets are held by a trustee and the owners or contributors of capital (the beneficiaries) possess evidences of ownership known as certificates of beneficial interest. Like a partnership, the owners may be personally liable to creditors unless the latter are on notice that they may look only to the trust assets for the settlement of their claims.

Depending on the nature of the trust declaration and the laws of the state, a trust of this kind *may* enjoy the status of a corporation, with limited liability to creditors, and in most cases it is subject to the Federal income tax applicable to corporations.

OTHER TRUSTS

There are many other kinds of trusts in addition to the more common ones described above. Most of these are more in the nature of business purpose trusts than private trusts, but they are probably worth a brief mention here for the sake of completeness.

A Real Estate Investment Trust offers important advantages to small investors. Under a set of very comprehensive tax rules, there is usually little or no tax on the trust, so the investors' profit is not cut down by an additional levy as it would be with a corporation. The trust property is generally real estate and the beneficiaries are the investors.

An Ohio Land Trust is one very similar to a real estate investment trust, with a few minor technical differences.

An Investment Trust is also much like a real estate trust except that securities rather than real estate are dealt with.

A Liquidating Trust is one organized for the primary purpose of liquidating and distributing the assets transferred to it.

Voting Trusts, bondholders protective committees, and other agencies formed to protect the interests of security holders during insolvency, bankruptcy, or corporate liquidations are similar to liquidating trusts.

There are a number of kinds of "Employee Trusts," usually subject to very strict tax rules, such as a Pension Trust for receiving and handling a company's pension deductions and contributions, a Profit Sharing Trust for the same purpose, an Employees' Stock Ownership Trust for receiving a company's stock to be held for later distribution to its employees, a Stock Bonus Trust, and others.

A Self-Employed Retirement Trust may be used by a person making contributions under a Keough plan, and an Individual Retirement Trust may be used by an employee establishing an individual retirement account.

An Accumulation Trust is simply one in which the income is to be retained by the trust rather than being distributed, generally for a certain length of time or until a certain event occurs. At one time these trusts produced income tax savings because the income would have been subject to a higher rate if it had gone to the creator of the trust or the beneficiary instead of accumulating in the trust. However, that advantage was restricted by a 1969 change in the law regarding the taxation of accumulation distributions.

A Foreign Trust is a trust whose income from sources outside the United States is not included in its gross income for tax purposes unless it is effectively connected with a United States trade or business.

Despite the many kinds of trusts mentioned in this chapter, this list should not be considered complete. There are probably a number of others, not very generally used. And, no doubt, there will surely be more and more kinds of trusts in the future as people discover and devise other uses for this versatile and flexible way of handling and transferring property.

3

THE TRUSTEE'S DUTIES AND RESPONSIBILITIES

It is obvious from the discussion of trusts up to this point that the trustee is a key figure, as well as a necessary one, in any trust.

A good trustee, one able to do whatever job is required by the particular trust, is an absolute necessity for a good, effective trust administration. The duties vary greatly in different trusts; sometimes very little is required of the trustee, but in other cases the administration could be a full time job requiring much knowledge and ability. And although a trustee's operations are sometimes under the supervision of the court, his day-to-day decisions can have very important consequences, and they could possibly result in unnecessary expense and difficulties even though he might have done nothing really illegal.

So naming the right person for the job is important, and a grantor planning a trust should give some thought to just what will be required of his trustee. Perhaps a close look at the duties and responsibilities of trustees in general would be helpful to a grantor in learning more about the position and in deciding just which person would be a good trustee in his particular case.

POWERS OF THE TRUSTEE

A trustee has only those powers given to him by a grantor and those vested in him by statute, rules of equity, or court orders. The grantor's intent in respect to his trustee's power and authority may be expressly stated in the trust instrument or may be implied in the general language of the instrument and the purposes of the trust. Historically, trustees' powers have been narrowly construed, but the current trend is to enlarge them. Most states now have statutes that confer some additional powers on the trustee, and a few states have enacted legislation with comprehensive lists of powers that apply to all trustees.

In general, the trustee will be considered to have all powers "necessary and appropriate" to carrying out the purposes of the trust, even though not specifically given to him, unless any are forbidden by the terms of the trust.

One of the most important powers a trustee could have would be the power to sell the trust property. If the trust instrument gives or withholds this power, that, of course, governs. But when the instrument is silent there is a conflict of opinion as to whether or not the power to sell is one of those "necessary and appropriate" powers. So a grantor should consider this in creating a trust and make his wishes clear in the trust instrument. Most often, the power to sell should be granted, especially where the trust consists of property of fluctuating and perhaps perishable value, such as corporate stocks. Also, changing situations years after the creation of the trust might make it very desirable for the trustee to be able to dispose of certain property, which he could not do if his hands were tied by the restrictions in the trust instrument.

A trustee's power to lease the trust property follows the same rules as his power to sell, but if he does have leasing powers he may not grant a lease for longer than the fixed term of the trust.

If the instrument is silent regarding borrowing against the trust property, there is generally no such power implied. However, a court might authorize borrowing in emergencies if it seemed desirable in order to preserve the trust estate and is consistent with the grantor's probable intent.

A trustee does have the implied power to incur reasonable expenses in the administration of the trust, including the power to make improvements on property when necessary to preserve the assets.

DUTIES OF THE TRUSTEE

Subject to the general rules and any specific limitations, a trustee's powers are very broad. Still, they are accompanied by many duties.

He has the duty, of course, to administer the trust in accordance with its terms. He must do this with the degree of care and skill which a "reasonably prudent businessman" would use in dealing with his own property, and, if he has any special skills, he is expected to use them as well.

In administering the trust, the trustee's primary duty is to preserve the trust property rather than to make it produce income, but since the purpose of most trusts is the production of income, that follows closely as another prime objective.

A trustee has a duty to keep his own funds and assets entirely separate from those of the trust; he cannot make a personal loan to the trust and he cannot borrow from the trust, even if he agrees to pay interest on the loan.

He may not accept any bonus or commission from any third person for any of his actions in connection with the trust.

A trustee has many other duties, most of which are described in following sections, and when he has breached any of his duties the beneficiary may take legal action against him to remove him from office, to compel his performance, or to recover damages from him.

Since a trustee has so much power and responsibility, and since there is always a possibility of having to recover damages from him, it is not at all uncommon for a grantor to require that his trustee be bonded. (This is an expense of the trust, not of the trustee.) And some states require bonding in certain cases, even though the grantor may have said that no bond was necessary.

OBTAINING THE PROPERTY

After the trustee has accepted the trust and qualified by taking an oath, giving bond, or taking any other steps required by law or the trust instrument, he has a duty to examine the trust terms to ascertain the property comprising its subject matter, the identity of the beneficiaries, and his own duties as trustee. He next has a duty to take tangible real or personal property into his possession and to take the steps necessary to secure the ownership of any documents representing intangible assets, such as savings account passbooks. In doing so he may make whatever use of agents and others as is reasonable in view of the type of property and the other circumstances of the case.

He must use reasonable diligence to discover the location of the trust property and to take control of it without unnecessary delay. If the trust is created by the grantor during his lifetime, the grantor will ordinarily deliver the trust property to the trustee at the time of the trust creation, but if he does not the trustee must hold the grantor to this obligation. If the trust is set up by will, the property will come to the trustee through the executor, and the trustee must require the executor to turn over the assets to him as soon as the will and probate law permit.

As part of his duty to assume control of the trust property, the trustee has the duty of collecting notes, bonds, mortgages, checks, or other contract or tort claims which are part of the trust estate. He will be personally responsible if he fails to use reasonable skill and diligence in fulfilling this duty.

Where the same person is executor and trustee under a will, it is often difficult to ascertain at a given time whether the trust has been set up or whether the fiduciary was still acting in the capacity of executor. Something more than a mere mental decision by the executor-trustee should take place to mark the transfer, such as setting up a trustee account in the books or notifying the beneficiary that the trust has been established.

CARING FOR THE ASSETS

A trustee must use reasonable care and prudence in caring for the trust assets. He must see that deeds are recorded, carry adequate insurance on insurable property, rent a safe deposit box for the care of securities and other important documents, and take any other action necessary to preserve the property against theft or other loss.

Cash funds should be kept in a sound banking organization, but of course it would be unwise to place more than $40,000, the federally insured amount, in any one account.

And the trustee should do anything else which a prudent man would do in caring for assets, such as inspecting them from time to time, supervising all investments, paying off encumbrances and taxes which might jeopardize title, keeping properties in good repair, and others.

MANAGEMENT OF THE ASSETS

A trustee has a duty to make the trust property produce income, so he must develop a program to secure income from the assets or to sell any non-productive assets (if he has this power) and reinvest the proceeds in other assets which do produce.

If there is land in the trust, it should be leased or otherwise made productive; if there is personalty it, too, should be made to produce income. And even cash should, for example, be kept in a savings account which pays interest rather than being kept in a nonproductive demand deposit account.

As for the types of investments a trustee may make, a few states still have "legal lists" of approved investments for trusts, sometimes mandatory, sometimes permissive. But most states now follow the "prudent investor rule" under which the trustee must only use good faith, sound discretion, and care in investing trust funds.

As for the propriety of certain kinds of investments under these rules, it is generally recognized that obligations issued or guaranteed by the United States or its instrumentalities are the safest investments for trustees. Also highly regarded are first mortgage loans on real property where the debt does not exceed a certain proportion of the value of the mortgaged property. Second mortgages or unsecured loans of any kind are usually held to be improper investments. Certain corporate bonds, secured by a mortgage to a trustee for the benefit of the bondholders, are commonly acceptable investments. Corporate stocks, usually excluded from the "legal lists," are often considered permissible investments in other states, depending on the particular types of stocks involved. Investments in partnerships are improper for a trustee. An investment in land for speculation would be difficult to justify, but if the land was related to some other trust purpose it might be proper.

Again, safety in investment is the primary concern, and the laws of the various states make an effort to insure this.

The trustee is personally liable to the beneficiaries for any loss or depreciation in value of the property due to his breach of trust, so he must be extremely careful in the matter of investments and must be certain that he conforms with his state's laws when making investments. It has even been held that if a grantor conveys property to the trustee which is not a proper trust investment, or if an investment later becomes improper through changes in the law or in economic conditions, the trustee is under an immediate duty to dispose of the property.

LOYALTY TO THE BENEFICIARIES

There are many ways in which the trustee, with his great power over the trust assets, might take advantage of his position to enrich himself, but the law has developed a standard of loyalty in trust relations which does not permit a trustee to create or occupy a position in which he has interests to serve other than the interest of the trust. Undivided loyalty is absolutely required, and the penalties visited upon the disloyal trustee can be uncommonly severe.

The trust must be administered solely for the benefit of the beneficiaries, and the trustee is not permitted to take any position which could conceivably be adverse to theirs. He must never obtain any personal advantage at the expense of the trust estate. If he has any personal dealings with the beneficiaries, he owes them a duty of utmost fairness, and the burden of proving this is on the trustee. He may not engage personally in any financial transactions involving the trust property, and he may not make loans to, or borrow from, the trust.

These self-interest rules are so strict that a corporate trustee cannot invest trust funds in its own stock and, in most states, it cannot even retain such shares if placed in the trust by the grantor. Nor can a bank-trustee generally keep trust funds on deposit in its own bank—though a number of states do now permit this.

The trustee is under a duty of absolute loyalty to the beneficiaries, and the law is extremely zealous in enforcing this principle.

USE OF DISCRETION

In the exercise of whatever powers may have been given to him by the grantor and by law, the trustee is generally considered to have discretion as to whether or not to use these powers. If, however, he is required to take certain actions (as, for example, to make periodic distributions), he has no discretion at all and must exercise the power conferred; if he fails or refuses to exercise his discretion the court may direct him to do so.

In addition to the normal discretionary powers trustees have in general, extraordinary discretion might be granted to some trustees. These would include such powers as deciding how much to distribute to a beneficiary, when to make a distribution, whether or not to favor one beneficiary over another, whether to invade the trust assets for a beneficiary's benefit, when to terminate the trust, and many others. The purposes of the trust, and the kind of trust it is, would dictate the amount and kind of discretion a grantor would give his trustee. But, as mentioned earlier, the granting of certain discretionary powers might insure against the disruptive effects of unforeseen future events and conditions.

DELEGATION OF AUTHORITY

A grantor chooses a trustee because of **confidence** in his judgment and integrity. From this premise evolved the rule that a trustee cannot delegate the performance of his trust duties. Yet a trustee cannot reasonably be expected to perform personally every act necessary to achieve the objectives of the trust. A grantor would not expect this, and a court should not enforce it.

The general rule is that a trustee, invested with powers, the execution of which calls for the exercise of discretion and judgment on his part, cannot delegate such power to anyone, and that the performance of any act requiring the exercise of discretion must be done by the trustee, unless the grantor expressly provides that the trustee may delegate the powers.

The trustee may, however, delegate the authority to perform a purely mechanical or "ministerial" act, that is, an act not requiring the exercise of discretion. He will often have to act through agents or attorneys, as well as through ministerial or clerical helpers, and if he determines in his own mind how to exercise the discretion and appoints others to carry out his determination he cannot be said to delegate the trust. But a rather high standard of prudence is required in selection of employees and agents.

Since a corporate trustee can act only through its officers and employees, entrusting work to them is not delegation but rather the execution of the trust by the trustee itself.

If the trustee does delegate some duty which he cannot properly delegate and a loss results, the trustee is personally liable to the beneficiaries.

THE TRUSTEE'S LIABILITY

It is apparent from the preceding sections that a trustee has a great amount of responsibility and that there are many acts which could cause him to be personally liable to the beneficiaries. But it is also possible for a trustee to become liable to third persons.

He is subject to personal liability to third persons for torts committed by him or his agents or employees in the course of the administration of the trust to the same extent he would be liable if he owned the property himself. And he is potentially liable to all parties with whom he contracts in the course of the administration.

But he does not necessarily have to bear the loss in these cases. He has a right of indemnification against the trust so long as he did not act improperly in the tort or contract. And he will generally not be personally liable on a contract in the first place if he acted properly in making the contract and included a valid, explicit disclaimer in it.

Again, if a trustee fulfills his office with complete good faith and prudence he stands very little chance of personal liability; if he does not, his liability can be very great indeed.

PAYMENT OF EXPENSES

Another duty of a trustee is to pay the expenses of the trust promptly, as a good businessman would do, and not allow obligations to become delinquent.

These expenses include not only the necessary expenses of operating the trust—employee salaries, office supplies, office rent, recording fees, and other administrative expenses—but also expenses necessary in connection with the trust's property, such as insurance, repairs, taxes, lockbox rent, and others.

Theoretically, these expenses are those of the trustee himself, but if they are proper trust expenses the trustee is entitled to reimbursement for them from the trust. So, as a practical matter, the trust bears the expenses and the trustee does not; the trustee simply has the responsibility for seeing that they are taken care of.

PAYMENT OF DISTRIBUTIONS

Trustees are generally held to be under an absolute duty to make payments and distributions to the correct beneficiary, rather than merely to use good faith, ordinary care, and the advice of counsel. If a trustee pays trust income or principal to the wrong person because of forgery, confusion of identity, misapprehension about the meaning of the trust instrument, or other mistake, he will be required to make good the amount from his own property.

If the beneficiary is an adult of normal capacity, a prudent trustee will make payment to him personally and not to any representative; if a minor or incompetent, the trustee should make payment to a properly appointed guardian, unless he is authorized to "apply" the income for the beneficiary's benefit.

A trustee must generally make payment or distribution exactly as specified in the trust instrument, such as in cash or in kind, but a court might sometimes permit deviation from this if it can be shown to be in the best interests of the beneficiaries without defeating any important purpose of the grantor.

INCOME AND PRINCIPAL

Since there are two kinds of beneficiaries of every trust (income beneficiaries and principal beneficiaries, or remaindermen, though the two may be the same), it is extremely important for the trustee to maintain a careful segregation between the trust's income and its principal. Otherwise, proper amounts might not be retained for the remaindermen.

During the administration, the trustee will have receipts that must be credited to either income or principal and will make disbursements that must be charged to one or the other. In making his decision regarding each transaction, the trustee must follow the terms of the trust instrument. The grantor is free to name the recipients of the trust's income and principal, to define their respective interests, and to define exactly what receipts shall constitute income and what expenses shall be charged against income; the trustee cannot deviate from these directions.

However, most trust instruments are not very explicit, simply directing that "income" shall be paid to a certain party without defining just what receipts and what disbursements comprise this income. The laws of the various states give the trustee some guidelines to follow in these cases, and most states have even adopted a Uniform Principal and Income Act, or a Revised Principal and Income Act, spelling out the differences between income and principal in some detail.

But where the law is silent or obscure on a question of allocation, or if the trust instrument leaves such questions to the discretion of the trustee, the trustee must make his choice in a prudent manner consistent with his basic obligation of impartiality among the different beneficiaries.

Generally, however, trust income includes all ordinary receipts from the use or investment of the trust property, such as rents, dividends, interest, and so on; trust principal includes other receipts, as from the sale or exchange of assets (capital gains and losses), extraordinary dividends, and others. Expenses against income include all those which go to the production or collection of income (taxes, upkeep, interest, and insurance, for example), while those charged to principal are the ones that go to improvement or preservation of the trust corpus (such as losses on sales, property assessments, major repairs, and the like).

The problems of correct allocation of receipts and disbursements, particularly in connection with a number of specific items, are dealt with more fully in the chapters on trust accounting and trust taxation.

ADEQUATE ACCOUNTING RECORDS

The important segregation of income and principal is difficult, if not impossible, unless adequate records are kept. But there are also other reasons for a trustee to keep good accounting records for his trust.

The law requires every trustee to keep orderly and accurate accounts with regard to the trust principal and income received by him, but even if it were not required a trustee should establish records for his own protection, showing a complete list and exact description of the property he received as trustee; he must be in a position to furnish a beneficiary with information about the status of the trust at any time; and he must have the detailed information necessary for the preparation of any reports or accountings to the court or others.

Adequate records are considered so important that it has even been held that a provision in a trust instrument saying that the trustee need not keep accounts *may* manifest an intention not to create a trust.

The kind of accounts needed by any particular trust might be very simple, even informal, or they might be quite the opposite. Trusts vary a great deal in size and complexity, and in many cases a trustee would be well advised to consult an accountant for help in deciding exactly what kind of records would be advisable for his trust.

Complete information and suggestions about a trust's accounting system is given in Chapter 5.

COMPENSATION OF THE TRUSTEE

Trustees have a right to compensation for their services, even where not granted in the trust instrument, and the amount of this compensation will be fixed either by the terms of the trust instrument, by contract between the grantor and the trustee, by statute, or by court action.

If there is a contract on compensation, the trustee will be bound by it, and he will be bound by compensation terms in the trust instrument if he did not initially object to them.

Most states have legislation on the allowance of trustee compensation, which will govern in the absence of a contract or terms in the trust instrument. The most common type of law authorizes the court, in its discretion, to allow the trustee "reasonable compensation." The trustee will generally request a specific amount, and the court will grant that amount or whatever lesser amount it deems fair and reasonable.

A few states provide that the trustee is "entitled" to reasonable compensation and give him the power to collect his compensation annually from the trust property without court action.

Still other states have statutes which set forth, in varying degrees of detail, a schedule or scale of commissions or fees that are permitted a trustee. Most of these schedules grant the trustee a graduated percentage of trust income, typically five or six percent on the first $5,000 and a lesser percent on additional brackets. The trouble with income commissions is that they work a hardship on a trustee who holds unproductive or low yield properties, but most fee schedules meet this problem by awarding additional compensation based on some other criteria, such as commissions on the receipt of corpus (as high as five percent in some jurisdictions) or commissions on the distribution of corpus, either periodically or at the termination of the trust (from one to two and a half percent in various jurisdictions). Another alternative is an annual commission based on the fair market value of the trust corpus. Such commissions are also graduated downward, with a rate of one-half of one percent on the first $50,000 of corpus being a typical maximum rate, with lesser amounts specified in states where a corpus commission is not the principal source of trustee compensation.

But, again, a grantor can override any statutory or judicial compensation arrangement by a contrary direction in the trust instrument; and a binding compensation contract will have the same effect.

Corporate trustees tend to avoid fixed-fee arrangements by insisting that the trust instrument include a clause granting them "reasonable compensation," or by specifying other guidelines susceptible of redefinition to meet changing conditions.

Unless otherwise provided by statute or in the trust instrument, a trustee cannot take his compensation until authorized by a court, usually in an accounting proceeding. This rule can, of course, work a financial hardship on trustees, and by lumping the payment of several years' compensation in a single year it can also have unfavorable tax effects on the trustee. So, in recent years, the trend has been toward statutes authorizing trustees to take their commissions annually without court authorization.

4

ACCOUNTINGS AND REPORTS TO THE COURT

A trustee had no common-law duty to file an inventory or other reports with the court, but some statutes have placed this obligation on some or all trustees. Many states now have comprehensive legislation governing the procedure on accountings. Generally, the trustee is required to account to the beneficiaries and the court at the time of termination of the trust, and he may be required to do so periodically during his administration.

In some states, formal court accounting is required annually or at some other specified interval, whether the beneficiaries have requested it or not. In other states no periodic accounting is required but the trustee may submit accounts when he desires to do so, and he must submit them when requested by a qualified beneficiary.

Many corporate trustees voluntarily file annual accounts in court, even though they have not been required to do so by statute, court rule, or court decree. They present complete information regarding their administration while it is fresh and current and thereby, in most cases, secure a court decree approving their accounts, thus removing all doubts as to their liability for the administration to that point. This would seem to be advisable for individual trustees as well.

Since a person accepting the position of trustee usually subjects all of his actions in connection with the administration of the trust to the review of the court, his knowledge that this is the case forces him to be more careful in complying with the governing statutes and the provisions of the trust instrument than he might be if he expected no such review.

The effect of such a system is that it emphasizes to the trustee that his position is a fiduciary one, and it strengthens the possibility that he will faithfully accomplish the objectives of his administration.

NECESSITY FOR PERIODIC ACCOUNTING REPORTS

Obviously the court does not actively supervise the day-to-day activities of any trustee. The court's review and control are accomplished, instead, by various statutory requirements making it mandatory for the trustee to file with the court periodic reports and accountings of his stewardship. One of the first and most important duties of a trustee is to keep and render full and accurate accounts concerning the trust in his hands.

These reports, when filed by the trustee and passed on by the court, become a matter of public record, which any interested parties may examine and to which they may file objections, if desired. In many jurisdictions such an account is not immediately passed on by the court, but is first referred to an auditor or referee, whose report is subject to confirmation, modification, or rejection by the court. The auditor is generally empowered to take testimony and make findings of fact. Exceptions to his report may be filed by either the trustee or any other interested person.

Many courts do not pretend to make a thorough study of a trustee's reports, but more or less rely on objections being filed by anyone believing himself to have been injured by improper acts of the trustee.

The court also needs a report from the trustee so that it can review the disbursements made by the trustee, for the purpose of determining whether the trustee is entitled to reimbursement for these expenditures. Theoretically, the trustee's expenditures are considered as having been made from his own personal funds but, if they are approved, he is reimbursed for them by being permitted to deduct them from the amount of the trust's cash for which he is accountable. The court will permit the trustee to be reimbursed for, or credited with, all proper claims against the trust which he has paid and for all actual and necessary expenses incurred in good faith and with exercise of reasonable judgment in the management of the trust.

WHEN REPORTS ARE REQUIRED

Reports of the progress of the administration of the trust are made to the court as often as the trustee cares to make them, or upon order of the court, or as required by statute. If the administration is not completely settled at the end of the first year, the trustee is frequently required to make an accounting annually.

At the time of termination, a final report or accounting is always made. An exception to this requirement may sometimes be permitted if all the beneficiaries make and file an agreement with the court which makes the accounting unnecessary.

INTERIM REPORTS

Any report or accounting made to the court prior to final settlement is known as an interim report.

It is good practice for the trustee to prepare an interim report at the end of each year of the administration, even though he may not be required to do so. It is well to have the approval of the court, or to learn of any objections, periodically as the administration progresses rather than wait until too late.

Reports covering each twelve-month period from the date of the creation of the trust are acceptable, but equally acceptable, and usually much easier to prepare, are reports covering periods corresponding to those covered by the fiduciary income tax returns; that is, the first report may include a period of less than a year (from the date of creation to the end of the trust's first fiscal or calendar year), and each succeeding report will cover a full twelve-month period, except that the final report may again be for less than one year. Trust books, like those of most businesses, are closed only at the end of each annual tax or accounting period, at which time any figures needed for reports are easily available either in summary form or in detail. Attempting to gather such information at some odd date in the middle of the accounting year is unnecessarily difficult.

THE FINAL REPORT

The court might accept a final report from the trustee covering only the period which has elapsed since the date of his most recent interim report, but a final report must generally cover the entire period of administration—from the date of the creation of the trust to the date of termination. This may cover a number of years, but its preparation should pose no particular problem, particularly if interim reports have been filed; such interim reports can easily be combined into a final, over-all report. (Of course, if the life of the trust has been very long, such as twelve, fifteen, twenty years or more, an exception would certainly be made.)

The effect of a final accounting is to close the trust and discharge the trustee. The court will examine the trustee's final report and determine whether or not the various expenditures listed therein are proper charges to the trust for which the trustee may be reimbursed or credited. It will also hear and rule on any objections which may be raised by creditors or beneficiaries. If everything is in order, the court will then issue a decree of distribution and discharge the trustee and cancel his bond.

FORM OF REPORT

There is no uniformity whatsoever as to the proper form for a trustee's interim or final reports. Most statutes have very little to say about just what kind of report shall be filed, frequently describing it in very general terms, such as "a statement of receipts and disbursements," but without specifying whether a detailed listing is required or whether a summary will suffice.

Each court is likely to have its own ideas about the format and content of a report. Some may insist on one certain form, others may accept any form which will present the information they need in making their review. It is advisable, therefore, for the trust's accountant to ask the judge or lawyer about the court's requirements before spending time preparing a report which will not be acceptable to that court. (This will often be a frustrating experience for an accountant because many courts will insist on reports in a much less informative form than the accountant would otherwise normally prepare.)

Generally, however, a summary cash statement must be prepared, accompanied by detailed schedules of cash receipts and cash disbursements.

Cancelled checks supporting the disbursements must often be presented to the court also. If the volume of transactions was very large, the detailed schedules might not be required, though the court might later ask for them if more detailed information is needed.

A desirable feature of any trustee's report (though not always required by the court) is for it to show, in some way, the disposition of all trust property which came into the trustee's hands. The beginning inventory of trust property plus gains and income and less losses, expenses and distributions, should be shown to equal the closing list of property being held for final distribution.

Another desirable feature, of course, is for the report to show separately the trust's operating income and expenses rather than have them intermingled with receipts and disbursements having to do with the principal of the trust (receipts from sales of assets, disbursements for administrative expenses, and the like). As mentioned earlier, a careful segregation of principal and income is important not only in the report but also in the accounting system, because the income beneficiaries are often not the same people who will receive the trust corpus. This is explained more fully in the chapter on trust accounting.

There is very little to guide the trustee or his accountant or lawyer in deciding on the best form for the reports, but it would seem that a "Charge and Discharge Statement," highly recommended for estate executors, would be the best for a trustee also; both are fiduciaries, both have the same kind of responsibility and accountability, and both are concerned with the proper segregation of income and principal. This form will serve for either interim or final reports, and it is acceptable to most courts.

A charge and discharge statement shows the trustee as being charged with all assets and funds which come under his control—the original assets, gains on sales, trust income, and so forth. There is deducted from this total the disbursements for which the trustee claims credit—the losses on sales, operating expenses, distributions paid, and other expenditures. The balance is the amount with which the trustee is still charged, and it must be represented by cash and other assets still in his possession.

It is preferable to divide a charge and discharge statement into two parts. One should be a statement covering only items relating to the principal of the trust, the other a statement covering only the trust's income and the expenses against that income. Each will show a closing balance and the total of the two balances will agree with the amount of the current listing of assets on hand.

To summarize, trustees' reports might take any one of many different forms, depending on the legal requirements, the wishes of the governing court, and the size and nature of the trust. The most simple kind of cash statement might suffice for a very small trust. For larger trusts, more formal and more complete reports are desirable. In any case, the charge and discharge statement recommended by most accounting writers is the most satisfactory type of report. But, unfortunately, its use is still far from universal, due largely to many courts being unfamiliar with any accounting statement other than a cash receipts and disbursements statement, and insisting on some less informative type of report.

REPORTS ILLUSTRATED

A simple cash receipts and disbursements statement, which might serve as an interim or a final report for a small trust, is shown in the following form.

JOHN K. FRANKLIN TRUST

Wilson Johnson, Trustee

STATEMENT OF CASH RECEIPTS AND DISBURSEMENTS

For the Year Ended December 31, 1977

Cash in Bank, January 1, 1977		$ 2,000.00
Receipts:		
Rental Income	$11,800.00	
Dividends on Stock	3,000.00	
Interest Income	1,600.00	
Total Receipts		16,400.00
Total Cash Accountable		$18,400.00
Disbursements:		
Repairs to Rental Property	$ 973.60	
Real Estate Taxes	1,462.50	
Personal Property Taxes	78.00	
Insurance on Property	426.00	
Lock Box Rental	14.25	
Trustee's Commission	700.00	
Distributions to Beneficiary	12,000.00	
Total Disbursements	15,654.35	
Balance, Cash in Bank, December 31, 1977		$ 2,745.65

Although the above report might be accepted by some courts, it has a serious deficiency in that it makes no mention of the trust assets and furnishes no accounting for them. A much more informative report could be made as follows, with the foregoing statement of receipts and disbursements being attached to it as a supporting schedule.

JOHN K. FRANKLIN TRUST

Wilson Johnson, Trustee

ANNUAL ACCOUNTING

For the Year Ended December 31, 1977

Trust Assets, January 1, 1977:

Cash in Bank	$ 2,000.00	
Land and Building	90,000.00	
500 Shares White Corp. Stock	50,000.00	
U.S. Government Bonds	32,000.00	
Total Assets		$174,000.00
Add: Cash Receipts, per Schedule		16,400.00
Total		$190,400.00
Deduct: Cash Disbursements, per Schedule		15,654.35
Balance, Trust Assets, December 31, 1977		$174,745.65

Consisting of:

Cash in Bank	$ 2,745.65	
Land and Building	90,000.00	
500 Sh. White Corp.	50,000.00	
Government Bonds	32,000.00	
Total	$174,745.65	

If the beginning or closing asset lists are very lengthy, they could be listed in separate schedules and only the totals shown on the statement.

The above statement with its supporting cash schedules adequately reports on the trust administration and is in a form which should be easily understood by most people. It still fails to show one important bit of information, however. It makes no distinction between transactions applying to the principal of the trust and those applicable to the trust's income.

This can be corrected by making a segregation of the receipts and the disbursements, as follows:

Add: Cash Receipts, per Schedule:		
Income Receipts	$16,400.00	
Principal Receipts	—	$16,400.00
Deduct: Cash Disbursements, per Schedule:		
Disbursements of Income	$15,304.35	
Principal Disbursements	350.00	$15,654.35

CHARGE AND DISCHARGE STATEMENT

Although the above type of statement might be preferred by many courts, it is still a very poor substitute for the recommended charge and discharge statement. A charge and discharge statement lends itself not only to reporting on a large trust but is adaptable to a trust of any size. As an illustration, page 73 shows a typical charge and discharge statement, using the same small trust that was used in the preceding examples.

PETITIONS TO THE COURT FOR INSTRUCTIONS

The court does not exist just for the purpose of protecting the beneficiaries from improper acts of the trustee. It also benefits and protects the trustee.

One of the most effective ways to enforce trusts is to avoid or discourage breaches of trust by clarifying the meaning of the trust instrument when the rights and duties it creates are not clear. The court has the right to give instruction on the rights, powers, and duties of the parties to a trust, and the trustee may even have a duty to seek such instruction when he cannot make a decision and inaction involves serious risk to the trust.

But the court will not advise a trustee as to his powers where they are clearly fixed by the trust instrument or by law; it will not advise the trustee how to exercise a discretion that the grantor has vested in him. There must be a legal problem of current importance to the trust concerning the meaning or legal effect of the trust instrument or the applicable law.

If there is such a problem, the trustee should not hesitate to ask for help. A written petition should be made to the court, and in these cases the court's reply will be in the form of a court order containing the information requested. A court order protects the trustee, and although he does not generally need such an order in the ordinary discharge of his duties, he should not hesitate to obtain this protection to cover any acts which are not clearly within his authority as granted by the statutes and the trust instrument.

JOHN K. FRANKLIN TRUST
Wilson Johnson, Trustee
CHARGE AND DISCHARGE STATEMENT
For the Year Ended December 31, 1977

First as to Principal:

The Trustee Charges Himself With:
Assets Placed in Trust (Schedule A) $174,000.00

The Trustee Credits Himself With:
Commission Allocable to Principal   350.00

Leaving a Balance of Principal of $173,650.00

Consisting of:		
Cash in Bank	$ 1,650.00	
Land and Building	90,000.00	
500 Sh. White Corp. Stock	50,000.00	
U.S. Government Bonds	32,000.00	
Total	$173,650.00	

Second as to Income:

The Trustee Charges Himself With:		
Rental Income	$ 11,800.00	
Dividends on Stock	3,000.00	
Interest Income	1,600.00	$ 16,400.00

The Trustee Credits Himself With:		
Rental Property Expenses	$ 2,862.10	
Other Property Expenses	92.25	
Commission Allocable to Income	350.00	
Distributions to Beneficiary	12,000.00	15,304.35

Leaving a Balance of Income of $ 1,095.65

Consisting of:
Cash in Bank $ 1,095.65

Schedule A — Assets Placed in Trust:

Cash	$ 2,000.00
Land and Building	90,000.00
500 Sh. White Corp. Stock	50,000.00
U.S. Government Bonds	32,000.00
Total	$174,000.00

5

TRUST ACCOUNTING
SIMPLIFIED

There is no standard accounting system for a trust. Trusts vary so very much in size and complexity that the books for each trust must be designed with that particular trust in mind. There are no standard or required bookkeeping forms which any trust must use. As a result, there could be, and probably should be, as much variation in the accounting systems for different trusts as there is in those for a small retail store and a large manufacturing company.

Many trusts are so small that it would, frankly, be a waste of time to even establish any set of books at all; for example, the only trust asset might be a single block of stock, the only income a dividend check twice a year, and the only disbursements a few checks for the trustee's fee, lock box rent, a distribution to a beneficiary, or others. But other trusts might contain many and varied assets and have a multitude of daily transactions, and a formal, efficient accounting system would be an absolute necessity for the protection of the trustee, for making the necessary reports, for proof of the proper handling of the transactions, and so on.

But regardless of the size of the trust or the complexity of the accounting system, the principles of trust accounting must be followed, and even the trustee who actually needs no formal bookkeeping system at all must understand these principles and keep them in mind and follow them in the administration of his trust.

If a bookkeeping system is to be established, an accountant should have no difficulty in doing the job if he keeps in mind the fact that trust accounting is basically just the same as any other accounting and that the only cause of difficulty is its relative unfamiliarity to most accountants. There are really only two or three points of difference which the accountant needs to know and understand to be able to design and maintain just as good a bookkeeping system for a trust as he could for any other business entity.

This discussion of trust accounting, therefore, dwells less on specific forms to be used than on the theory and principles of trust accounting, in the belief that the accountant on the job is the best man to design the actual accounting system—provided he knows and understands just what the system must accomplish.

The discussion is directed to the accountant establishing a system for an individual trustee rather than for a corporate trustee. Corporate trustees have their own accounting systems, of course, which differ greatly from what is described in this chapter—though their systems must also follow the same basic principles and attain the same objectives as those of individual trustees.

Nor is it contemplated that the suggestions and procedures given in this chapter will serve for Business Trusts, Real Estate Investment Trusts, Pension Trusts, and the like, but rather for the kinds of trusts that have current income beneficiaries and principal beneficiaries whose interests may be and generally are separate.

SPECIAL TRUST ACCOUNTING REQUIREMENTS

The principal problem encountered in designing and maintaining the accounts for a trust is the absolute necessity of having the books distinguish clearly between the principal (or corpus) of the trust and its income. This is explained more fully in the following section.

The next problem which the accountant must keep in mind is that the books of the trust must produce, at the end of each accounting period, a figure known as *Fiduciary Accounting Income.* This may seem overly obvious, but it is not. Fiduciary accounting income does not mean accounting income in the ordinary sense of the term but is the net income determined in exact accordance with whatever specific directions might be contained in the trust instrument (or state law) for the trust the system is being designed for. Income tax considerations must be ignored completely,a nd this does present a difficulty for accountants, who are generally so tax-conscious. The reasons and logic for this requirement will be explored later.

And finally, there is the problem of determining exactly how to make the accounting system accomplish the objectives just mentioned, and the remainder of this chapter should be helpful in this respect.

HOW TO HANDLE TRANSACTIONS AFFECTING PRINCIPAL AND INCOME

The main point of difference between trust accounting and ordinary accounting is caused by the necessity for keeping the books in such a way as to distinguish clearly between the principal (or corpus) of the trust and its income.

The distinction between principal and income is required because in most cases the trust instrument designates one person, or several people, to receive the income (a life tenant, perhaps), and another to receive the principal at some future time (a remainderman). This is common in both inter-vivos and testamentary trusts. So the books that the trustee is responsible for must be kept in such a way that at any time the amount accruing to each of the two classes of beneficiaries may be determined.

A simple example might help to clarify the differences between transactions affecting principal and those affecting income. Suppose a trust consists solely of non-income producing property—a vacant house, its furnishings, a vacant lot, and cash in the bank. If the vacant lot is sold for the amount at which is was placed in trust, one asset (the lot) is simply exchanged for another (cash or a receivable), and neither principal nor income is affected. If the lot is sold for more than its book figure, the terms of the trust instrument or state law must be consulted to see whether such a gain is to be considered as income or as an increase in the principal of the trust. The terms of the trust instrument govern in such a case, but if it is silent the law of the state will govern. If cash is spent in paying administration expenses, the effect on income or on principal will, again, be determined by the provisions of the trust instrument or state law.

But suppose that the residence is rented to a tenant; the rent received is income. Suppose the proceeds from the sale of the vacant lot are invested in bonds; the interest on the bonds is income though the bonds themselves remain a part of the principal.

Suppose, further, that the net income accumulates in an amount which warrants its investment, and it is invested in bonds. These bonds do not become principal, they are still a part of the assets belonging to income.

The legal theory seems to be that the principal of a trust is not a certain amount of monetary value, but is a certain group of assets which must be capable of isolation from the assets which compose the undistributed net income. These assets of the principal may change in form, or even in amount, but they always constitute the principal of the trust.

Actual separation of cash and other assets between those belonging to principal and to income is difficult, however. But it will ordinarily be sufficient to keep one account for cash and one for each type of investment, and to indicate the claims of the principal and the income in the total. This can be accomplished by a carefully planned chart of ledger accounts. Those accounts representing receipts of income minus those representing deductions from income gives the amount of the net income, which will be the amount of the assets making up the undistributed income. It is relatively unimportant just which specific assets comprise this amount, but the more liquid assets will generally be so designated—cash and any securities purchased with net income.

A device recommended by most accountants as an aid in the proper segregation of principal and income is the use of two separate ledger accounts for cash (although there is only one bank account and one checkbook). Each journal will have a pair of columns for these accounts, "Principal Cash" and "Income Cash." This forces the accountant to make a decision regarding the proper segregation of principal and income each time any receipt or disbursement is entered in the journals. It also results in the ledger accounts showing how much of the asset, cash, belongs to principal and how much belongs to income.

To summarize, the amount of the trust's net income must be carefully built up in the accounts, transactions affecting the trust principal rather than income must be recognized and excluded from income, and some way must be found of identifying the assets into which this net income has found its way.

This represents no radical change from ordinary commercial accounting; it is, rather, just a shift in emphasis. An accountant keeping this in mind should have no great trouble with trust accounting.

FIDUCIARY ACCOUNTING INCOME

The creator of a trust may spell out any terms and conditions he desires for the operation of that trust. The operation of the trust and its accounting system must be in complete conformity with any such provisions in the trust instrument, and the books must, therefore, produce the figures contemplated by the trust grantor.

Most often, the grantor's prime concern will be the amount of income which he wants the trust to produce for the benefit of some beneficiary, but his idea of what constitutes "income" may be far different from what is income in the general accounting sense or what is income for tax purposes. Still, his directions must govern, and the trust's books must show as net income whatever the grantor has directed. This figure is known as *fiduciary accounting income,* and is the correct income for *that particular trust.* The fiduciary accounting income for any other trust could be very different; ordinary accounting income could be very different; and almost invariably taxable income will also be very different.

But it cannot be overemphasized that the accounts for any trust must be designed to show the (sometimes very peculiar) income which the grantor of that trust had in mind. This is the income he intended for the beneficiary to receive and, again, his wishes must be followed. If the books are kept in accordance with these principles, the trustee's responsibility and accountability to the income beneficiary, as well as to the remainderman, will be clear at all times. The trustee is governed by the terms of the trust instrument, and a good accounting system will be an invaluable aid to him in properly administering the trust.

Obviously, fiduciary accounting income will almost never be the same as the taxable income which the accountant will be concerned with later. But tax considerations must be ignored completely at this point. As will be demonstrated later, adjustments will have to be made to arrive at taxable income, but the starting point in determining *taxable income* is always *fiduciary accounting income.*

CAPITAL GAINS AND LOSSES

There are several kinds of transactions, in particular, which are subject to different possible treatment in their effect on the principal or on the income of a trust, and one of these is gains and losses on the sale of trust property.

If the trustee has the power to sell some of the trust's property, he might do so at a price either greater or less than the value he was charged with as a part of the trust's principal. Is this gain or loss applicable to the trust's income or does it change the amount of the trust's principal? The trust instrument will govern; it might provide for either treatment. But unfortunately, many instruments fail to mention this, though it is an important provision to incorporate into any trust.

If the instrument does not answer this question, state law will give the answer. Each state has a statute defining, in more or less detail, what shall be considered principal and what income, and although these laws do not override any specific direction in a trust instrument they do control otherwise. So, depending on the circumstances in a particular case, the trust's fiduciary accounting income may be affected or the trust's principal amount may be changed. More often than not, it will be found that these gains and losses apply to principal, but this is certainly not always the case.

If such a transaction is applicable to principal rather than to income, this does not mean, however, that it can be ignored for income tax purposes. It is still a capital gain or loss on the fiduciary tax return, and this is one of the possibly many adjustments that will have to be used in bringing fiduciary accounting income down to a correct taxable income figure.

DEPRECIATION TREATMENT

Another item which might or might not affect the fiduciary accounting income is depreciation.

If there is depreciable or (depletable) property in the trust, should depreciation expense be charged and the decrease in value of the property be funded through a depreciation allowance as in ordinary accounting? This, again, depends on just what the trust instrument might have to say about it. If it mentions or provides for depreciation, this indicates that the trust grantor was aware of this and that he intended for the trust income to bear the expense of depreciation; the accounting system, then, must provide for it and fiduciary accounting income will be income after depreciation.

If the trust instrument is silent regarding depreciation, state law will govern. Most often, the laws provide for depreciation to be considered and charged against income, but otherwise depreciation must be ignored in the accounting system, and in this case the fiduciary accounting income will not be reduced by any depreciation.

But even if no depreciation is provided for in the trust's books, this does not mean that it cannot be used as a deduction for income tax purposes. Fiduciary accounting income will be adjusted for any allowable depreciation in arriving at taxable income.

TREATMENT OF VARIOUS SPECIAL RECEIPTS

The correct allocation of a trust's receipts between income or principal, to determine the correct fiduciary accounting income, seems to cause a little more difficulty than does the allocation of its disbursements, so these receipts will be considered in this section, with the disbursements being discussed in the following sections.

There are several transactions, not too frequently encountered, which the trust's accountant should be aware of because of their possible effect on the trust's income. These are seldom thought of by a grantor in creating a trust, but if they are, his directions will, of course, govern. Otherwise, state law will have to be consulted for the proper treatment as affecting the trust's principal or its income.

One such transaction is a corporate distribution of its own shares, such as a stock dividend or a stock split. This would, in practically all states, apply to principal. The same is true with stock rights and with liquidating dividends. Dividends made by a regulated investment company from its ordinary income apply to trust income, but those from capital gains, depletion, and the like are principal.

The amortization of premium or discount on bonds is usually ignored, and the proceeds from their sale or redemption is generally an increase or decrease in principal.

The proceeds from property taken on eminent domain proceedings and proceeds of insurance on losses of property constituting a part of principal will apply to the trust's principal.

There might be a number of other unusual but troublesome transactions demanding a decision as to their proper treatment. Again, a directive might be found in the statutes but, if not, the decision of the trustee, acting in good faith, will be upheld—and a trust instrument will often specifically give the trustee discretion in such matters.

Most receipts, however, cause little difficulty and are allocated as they would be in ordinary accounting practice. Common items applicable to income would include rents from real and personal property, interest on loans or notes or mortgages, interest on bank accounts or corporate or government bonds (including tax-exempt bonds), ordinary corporate dividends, income from a business or farming operation, income from a partnership or other fiduciary, and any other return in money or property derived from the use of the trust principal. Occasionally, an apportionment of income is necessary, as when a receipt includes income accrued to the date of death for a testamentary trust (which is principal) and that earned after death (income), or the accrual up to the date of creation of an inter-vivos trust (principal) and that accruing afterwards (income).

Receipts applicable to principal are those mentioned earlier as well as simple repayment of loans, sale of an asset of the principal, and any other profit or loss resulting upon any change in form of the principal.

EXPENSES APPLICABLE TO INCOME

The allocation of expenses as to income or to principal is usually in accordance with general accounting principles, but, as always, the grantor might have included some contrary provisions in the trust instrument, and these will govern in determining fiduciary accounting income.

But in the absence of specific directions in the trust instrument regarding any particular expense, state law should be examined. The laws vary from state to state, of course, but for the most part the expenses applicable to income include the ordinary expenses incurred in the administration, management, and preservation of the trust property, taxes on the property, insurance, interest, ordinary repairs, and so on; depreciation (if provided for); court costs, attorney fees, and other fees in proceedings if the matter primarily concerns the income interest; and income taxes levied on the trust's income.

As for the trustee's compensation and other overall administrative expenses (which might include office rent, clerk hire, and others), the trust instrument should say whether income or principal should be charged, but if it does not, many state laws simply say that one-half shall be charged to income, the remainder to principal. This group of expenses could be large enough to be of some importance, so a grantor should make the decision as to their allocation, but, unfortunately, it is overlooked in many trust instruments.

EXPENSES APPLICABLE TO PRINCIPAL

As for expenses chargeable against principal, state laws, in general, say they shall include the trustee's compensation and other administrative expenses not charged to income, special compensation of trustees, expenses incurred directly in connection with principal, court costs and fees primarily concerning matters of principal, and so on.

Also, principal charges include the costs of investing and reinvesting principal, payments on the principal of an indebtedness, and expenses in maintaining or defending any action to construe the trust or protect it or the property or to assure the title of the property.

And, of course, extraordinary repairs or capital improvements to the trust property, including special assessments, are proper charges to principal.

But a reminder—even though certain expenses are chargeable to principal under the terms of the trust instrument or state law for the correct determination of a particular trust's fiduciary accounting income, this does not necessarily mean they are not to be considered as expenses against income *for tax purposes*. Fees and administrative expenses, for example, are tax deductions even though they might be considered principal for trust accounting purposes, and such items are among the possibly many adjustments required to bring fiduciary accounting income to the correct taxable income.

The foregoing discussion of many of the possible transactions which can have important effects on the fiduciary accounting income of a trust should make it obvious that a trust grantor would be wise to give thought to as many of them as possible and make his wishes known in the trust instrument, unless he is willing to have his state's laws govern. Or, perhaps even better in the case of some transactions, he might give discretionary powers in the allocation of certain items to his trustee, who will be in a position to watch to trust work in the future.

ILLUSTRATIVE CHART OF ACCOUNTS FOR TRUSTS

With the preceding discussion of the general principles of trust accounting in mind, it might be well at this point to study an illustrative chart of the accounts which could be found in a trust's general ledger. It is highly unlikely, of course, that any one trust would need all of the accounts shown, but most of the ones possible for various trusts have been included for illustrative purposes.

A glance at the example given on page 84 will show that a trust's chart of accounts is very similar to one which any other business entity might use. The only real difference is that there are two net worth sections, one for Principal and one for Income.

Some of the individual account titles might seem unfamiliar, but these will be explained later. For the present, consider only the functions and interrelationships of the various groups of accounts shown by the chart.

ILLUSTRATIVE CHART OF ACCOUNTS

GENERAL LEDGER ACCOUNTS

Assets:

 100—Petty Cash
 101—Principal Cash
 102—Income Cash
 103—Notes Receivable
 104—Bonds
 105—Corporate Stocks
 106—Real Estate
 107—Allowance for Depreciation
 108—Partnership Interest
 109—Miscellaneous Assets
 110—
 111—

Liabilities:

 200—Notes Payable
 201—Mortgage Payable
 202—Payroll Tax Deductions
 203—
 204—

Net Worth (Principal):

 300—Trust Principal
 301—Additional Principal
 400—Gains Applicable to Principal
 401—Losses Applicable to Principal
 402—Administrative Expenses, Principal
 403—Dividends Applicable to Principal
 404—Distributions of Principal
 405—
 406—

Net Worth (Income):

 500—Trust Income
 600—Distributions of Income

Income:

 700—Tax Exempt Interest
 701—Taxable Interest
 702—Dividends Received

703—Rental Income
704—Partnership Income
705—Other Income
706—Gains Applicable to Income
707—
708—
709—
710—

Expenses:

800—Trustee's Fee
801—Salaries
802—Office Rent
803—Office Supplies
804—Telephone
805—Repairs
806—Insurance
807—Utilities
808—Real Estate Taxes
809—Payroll Taxes
810—Interest Expense
811—Travel Expense
812—Commission on Collections
813—Depreciation Expense
814—Miscellaneous Expenses
815—Income Taxes Paid
816—Losses Applicable to Income
817—
818—
819—
820—

The 100 series, Assets, will cause no difficulty. As with any asset section, accounts are set up for whatever property the trust owns plus any accounts expected to be needed (such as Allowance for Depreciation). The accounts may, of course, be listed in great detail or they may be condensed. For example, if the trust owns ten pieces of real estate, there could either be separate ledger accounts for each of the ten or one account including all of them. The only peculiarity in the asset section is the division of the usual cash account into two accounts, Principal Cash and Income Cash, as suggested earlier.

The liabilities section, 200 series, might never be used, as a trust usually starts out with no liabilities. And trust accounting is usually on a cash basis, so there is seldom any need for liability accounts on the books. In handling the business of the trust, however, some liabilities may be incurred, but these are usually current in character, such as a short-term note payable or payroll tax deductions. Any entries to this section will be made in accordance with ordinary accounting principles. But there is a possibility that some property subject to a mortgage might have been placed in trust, and the mortgage should, of course, be recorded as a liability in the opening entry along with the recording of the asset.

Account number 300, Trust Principal, is the equity account, the equivalent of an investment account or a capital stock account. The concept of proprietorship is almost entirely absent in trusts, and its place is taken by responsibility or accountability, the amount being determined by the adjusted balance in the Trust Principal account. It is this account which is credited with the total original amount of the property placed in trust, for which the trustee is accountable. Changes in the amount for which the trustee is responsible are recorded through entries to the various accounts in the 400 series. These accounts include the expenses which are applicable to Principal, transactions affecting Principal, and distributions of Principal. They will all finally be closed into the Trust Principal account, but this is not usually done periodically. These accounts are left open until the final closing of the books, at which time (after final distribution of the assets) they are closed into Trust Principal and should entirely eliminate the balance in the Trust Principal account. At any time prior to the final closing, the amount for which the trustee is responsible to the principal beneficiaries can be determined by combining the balances in all of the 300 and 400 series accounts. The net credit balance must be supported by net assets belonging to Principal.

Account number 301, Additional Principal, would be used only if there happened to be later additions of property to the trust. It might be just as well to credit these additions to account number 300, but by using a second account, the original account will always show the original balance of the trust's principal.

The other equity, or accountability, account is Trust Income. A credit balance in this account represents the trustee's responsibility to the income beneficiaries. This Trust Income account will never have an opening balance. Nothing can appear in it until income is earned. Income and the expenses applicable to income are accumulated in the accounts listed in the 700 and 800 series during each accounting period, and these accounts are closed into Trust Income at the end of each period—just as the nominal accounts of any other business are closed into Investment or Surplus periodically. If distributions are made to income beneficiaries, account number 600, Distributions of Income, is debited. This account remains open until the final closing, but, at any time, its balance, deducted from the balance in Trust Income, represents the undistributed income for whice the trustee is accountable. This amount must be supported by the physical assets (frequently cash only) belonging to Income.

Just as an ordinary investment account must always match the net assets of a business, so must the two trust equity accounts always equal the trust's net assets.

Reference should be made to the Charge and Discharge Statement illustrated in Chapter 4, and it will be seen how easily the set of accounts described above will lend themselves to the preparation of such a statement, whether it be an interim statement or a final accounting.

THE BOOKKEEPING SYSTEM

A very small trust might require no formal bookkeeping system at all. If only a few cash receipts are expected during the period of administration and if only a handful of checks will be written, a simple listing of receipts and disbursements will take the place of a set of books.

Larger and more complex trusts will, however, need formal accounting systems, and the style and complexity of these systems will depend on the volume and variety of transactions anticipated during administration.

The basic requirement for such a set of books, as in any accounting system, is a general ledger. The accounts to be set up in this ledger should be very carefully planned with a view to the probable future transactions to be embraced by these accounts. Reference should be made to the illustrative chart of accounts so that the titles which are peculiar to trusts will not be overlooked.

As with any accounting system, common sense and the accountant's good judgment will dictate the details of the chart of accounts finally decided on.

It might be found that subsidiary ledgers are desirable. For example, if the trust has numerous notes, mortgages, and accounts receivable, a receivables ledger would be necessary; if only two or three receivables existed, it might be more desirable simply to have a separate general ledger account for each. The same principles would apply in the case of securities, real estate, and miscellaneous assets.

As for the journals, great latitude is permitted in their design. A general journal is always desirable, however, for the entering of opening and closing entries, adjustments, corrections, and any other entries which do not readily lend themselves to columnar journals. The average medium-sized trust will usually need only one other book, a combination cash receipts and disbursements journal. The column headings for a journal of this kind might be as follows:

(Column)	(Account Number per Chart)
Date	
Payee or Explanation	
Check Number or Receipt Number	
Principal Cash—Debit	101
Principal Cash—Credit	101
Income Cash—Debit	102
Income Cash—Credit	102
Notes Receivable—Credit	103
Tax-Exempt Interest—Credit	700
Other Interest—Credit	701
Dividends Received—Credit	702
Rent Income—Credit	703
Other Income—Credit	705
Administration Expenses, Principal—Debit	402
Salaries—Debit	801
Office Rent—Debit	802
Office Expenses—Debit	803
Telephone—Debit	804
Repairs—Debit	805
Insurance—Debit	806
Utilities—Debit	807
Real Estate Taxes—Debit	808
Payroll Taxes—Debit	809
Interest Expense—Debit	810
Travel Expense—Debit	811
Miscellaneous Expense—Debit	814
Other Accounts—Account Number	
Other Accounts—Debit	
Other Accounts—Credit	

Column headings are set up for those accounts expected to be affected most frequently, of course. Entries to any other accounts will be made in the last three columns.

When the volume of transactions is very large, or when so many journal columns are needed that a combination journal would become unwieldy, this journal should be replaced by two others—a cash receipts journal and a cash disbursements journal.

The bookkeeping system described above, together with any necessary subsidiary ledgers and memorandum records, should serve for any trust, and it will be obvious that this system is basically the same as that which is used in any commercial business. The only real difference is the use of the two pairs of cash columns for the separation of principal cash and income cash instead of the usual one pair of columns.

One important fact should be kept in mind in designing the accounting system for a trust—trust books are almost invariably kept on the cash basis rather than the accrual basis, so no accounts need be set up for the many accruals usually necessary for an accrual-basis commercial business.

THE ACCOUNTING PERIOD

The accounting period for a trust is a twelve-month period. The trustee may elect a calendar year or a fiscal year ending on the last day of any month. Two factors might enter into the decision regarding the best fiscal year to select—the time of the year at which it will be most convenient to close the books and prepare income tax returns (natural business year) and the possible desirability of having a "short" accounting period from the date of inception of the trust to the end of the first fiscal year in order to have some of the trust's income taxed in a lower bracket than if a full year's income were reported at one time.

The journals are posted to the ledger each month, of course, and the ledger is closed at the end of each accounting period, at which time all income and expense accounts (700 and 800 series accounts) are closed into Trust Income. No other accounts are closed into the two net worth accounts, however, until the final closing of the books at the termination of the trust.

In short, the rules governing a trust's accounting period are exactly the same as for a corporation.

THE OPENING BOOKKEEPING ENTRY

The entry to open a trust's set of books is simple—debit each proper asset account for whatever property is placed in trust (with a related credit for accompanying mortgages, if any) and credit Trust Principal for the total.

But the determination of the proper *amounts* to use in this entry is not always simple at all. If the trust is a testamentary trust for a decedent dying before January 1, 1977, the property received from the decedent's estate takes a basis equal to its fair market value at the date of death—the figure established by the filing of the federal estate tax return—and this value should be used in the opening entry. Or, if no estate tax return had to be filed, the correct value is the one determined for state inheritance tax purposes. However, if the alternate date valuation was actually used on a federal estate tax return, that valuation would, of course, be the proper one. This method of determining the valuation to be used gives the trust a correct basis for the property for both income tax purposes and any other purposes. If the decedent died after December 31, 1976, the property's "carryover basis" should be used, as determined under the Tax Reform Act of 1976.

In the case of an inter-vivos trust, however, it must first be remembered that the transfer of property to the trust constitutes a gift, and the tax rules applicable to individual taxpayers may come into play. This means that, for tax purposes, the correct basis may not be known until many years after the gift was made; that is, if the property is sold at a gain the grantor's basis would be used, if sold at a loss the lower of the grantor's basis or fair market value at date of gift, and so on.

This makes an opening entry which will be correct in all cases for tax purposes an impossibility; but for fiduciary accounting purposes, it is general practice to record the property at its fair market value at the date of the transfer. And this is logical, because it is undoubtedly the present value of the property which the grantor has in mind when creating the trust; also, it is certainly the amount with which the trustee should be charged and be responsible for and upon which he should expect to produce income. If a later sale discloses that, for tax purposes, the valuation used in the opening entry was wrong, an adjustment will simply have to be made—for tax purposes. And the usual rules for holding period, adjustment for gift tax paid, and so on will apply.

BUSINESS INCOME

It is possible, of course, for a going business to be an asset of a trust. This is a little more common in the case of a testamentary trust, but a living trust can also be the recipient of a business and this is an asset which must be handled in the trust's accounting records.

The accountant has the choice of incorporating the bookkeeping system of the business into the trust's bookkeeping system or of continuing separate books for the business and using only a "control" account in the books of the trust.

Combining the two sets of books can cause numerous complications, so it is generally considered much more satisfactory to keep them separate.

The business interest will have been given an appraised valuation, and it is this figure which will be debited to an asset account, "Business Interest," in the opening entry. At the end of each accounting period of the business, the trust will debit this asset account for the amount of the business net profit and will credit an income account for the same amount. As the trust makes periodic withdrawals of cash from the business, the Business Interest account will be credited when income cash is debited on the trust books.

The accountant should be careful to determine if the business profits credited to trust income include any capital gains. If so, this income should be segregated into its two elements, ordinary income and capital gains, for proper fiduciary accounting treatment.

If a proprietorship business is acquired through a decedent's estate, the books of the business should be continued just the same as before the decedent's death, with one exception. It is highly unlikely that the net worth balance at date of death, as shown by the business books, will be the same as the appraisal figure in the estate inventory and, therefore, the trust's books, but these two figures must be made to agree. To accomplish this, the book values of the assets of the business will be adjusted to the appraisal figure. This is mandatory because these new valuations become the new tax and depreciation bases for the assets. This follows the principles mentioned earlier for determining the valuation at which to record trust assets. And following the same principles, a business given to an inter-vivos trust will also take a new valuation at which it will be recorded by the trust and to which the business assets should be adjusted.

One other point to remember is that the annual accounting period of the business must be changed to agree with that adopted by the trust, if the two are not already the same.

The above comments regarding a proprietorship interest are equally applicable to an interest in a partnership which is being continued with the trust taking the place of the partner. The appraised valuation of this partnership interest is set up as an asset on the trust books; the trust's share of net profits, determined at the end of the partnership's fiscal year, is a debit to this asset account and a credit to an income account, and cash withdrawals by the trust are debited to income cash and credited to the Partnership Interest asset account.

If the business is a corporation, none of the above applies, of course. The trust simply owns corporate stock and the corporation continues as a separate entity with no change in its bookkeeping.

DISTRIBUTIONS TO BENEFICIARIES

Income distributions to beneficiaries will cause no accounting difficulty. They are simply charged to the Distributions of Income account, but if there is more than one beneficiary it would be well to make notations in the ledger account of the names and amounts each time.

If distributions of principal are authorized, such distributions are debited to the Distributions of Principal account, and the total value of the principal is reduced accordingly.

The two distribution accounts will remain open on the books until the final termination of the trust, but their balances can be combined with their related Trust Principal and Trust Income accounts at any time to determine the current status and amount of the undistributed principal and income of the trust.

The same kind of entries should be made for the final distributions upon termination of the trust.

CHARITABLE DISTRIBUTIONS

A trust's donation to a charity is never treated as an expense; it would be improper for a trustee to burden income with such a payment, which is certainly not a proper operating expense. Contributions are, instead, distributions, and they are made only as provided for in the trust instrument.

But charitable distributions are quite common, and some trusts even provide for no distributions except charitable ones.

A charitable distribution may be made from income or from principal or both, depending on the terms of the trust instrument, and these terms will govern the accountant in recording the distribution—it will simply be charged to the proper distribution account, the same as a distribution to an individual beneficiary.

But charitable distributions may be treated as expenses for income tax purposes, whether made from income or from principal, and will be one of the items used in adjusting fiduciary accounting income to tax income, as will be explained in a later chapter.

THE PAYMENT OF INCOME TAXES

The income taxes paid by a trust on its net taxable income are considered as an operating expense rather than a charge against principal.

When paid, they are debited to an expense account. Of course, the trust instrument could provide otherwise, but it is more logical for income to bear the expense.

It might be argued that any portion of the income taxes attributable to income which was added to Trust Principal, such as capital gains, should be charged against principal rather than income, but, for practical purposes, this is very seldom considered.

ANNUAL CLOSINGS AND FINAL CLOSING

There are seldom any adjusting entries which need to be made at the end of each accounting period, because a trust is usually on the cash basis and accruals are unnecessary. There will, however, be an entry to record depreciation if depreciation is to be considered an expense for fiduciary accounting purposes.

As for the closing entry, all of the income and expense accounts (700 and 800 series) are closed into Trust Income (account 500). No other entries are necessary.

Upon final termination of the trust, adjusting entries, if any, will be made, followed by the same closing entry as for an annual closing. Next, the Distributions of Income account will be closed into Trust Income. This will be followed by an entry closing Additional Principal (account 301) and all of the accounts in the 400 series into Trust Principal (account 300).

If distribution of all assets has been made by this time, all accounts will now have a zero balance. If not, the Trust Income account will show the portion of the net remaining assets to be given to the income beneficiaries, and the Trust Principal account will indicate the amount to be turned over to the remainderman.

Obviously, the closing entries for a trust are almost identical with those for any other entity, the main difference, again, being the use of two proprietorship accounts instead of the usual one.

6

THE TAXATION OF TRUSTS

A trust is a distinct taxable entity and is, in most cases, required to file an income tax return on Form 1041, U.S. Fiduciary Income Tax Return.

The trustee is responsible for filing the return and paying any tax due, and he may become personally liable for his failure to pay the tax. It is incumbent on him to determine if a return must be filed for his particular trust and to learn of any other requirements in connection with the return filing.

The various requirements and the principles of trust income taxation in general are given in this chapter.

WHO MUST FILE A RETURN

A trustee must file a Form 1041 for his trust if the trust has *any* taxable income for the taxable year or if it has *gross* income of $600 or more regardless of the amount of taxable income. Also, if any beneficiary of the trust is a nonresident alien a return must be filed regardless of the amount of its income.

A person who is a trustee of more than one trust must file a separate return for each trust, even if the trusts were created by the same grantor for the same beneficiaries.

A separate employer identification number is required for each trust, and this number should be applied for (using Form SS-4) very soon after the creation of the trust, whether or not the trust expects to have any employees. It must be shown on all returns filed by the trust.

(The trustee of a charitable remainder trust or unitrust must make a return on Form 1041-B for each of the trust's taxable years.)

In addition to the Form 1041, the trustee will also have to file:

A Schedule K-1 for each beneficiary, showing that beneficiary's share of income, deductions, and credits, with a copy of this form going to the beneficiary.

Schedule D if there are any capital gains or losses.

Schedule J if there has been an accumulation distribution (see Chapter 10).

Form 1041-NR if there are any nonresident alien beneficiaries.

Forms 1096 for certain payments made by a trust engaged in a trade or business.

DOCUMENTS TO BE FILED

A trustee must file a notice of his fiduciary capacity with the District Director. Form 56 is used for this notice and is usually sent along with the trust's first tax return. (Upon termination of the trust the trustee should give notice that his fiduciary capacity has terminated, but there is no official form for this.)

If the gross income of the trust is $5,000 or more for the year, the tax return must be accompanied by a copy of the trust instrument (or the will in the case of a testamentary trust), and the trustee must attach a written declaration that it is a true and complete copy.

The trustee must also file a statement indicating the provisions of the governing instrument which, in his opinion, determine the extent to which the income of the trust is taxable to the trust, to the beneficiaries, to the grantor, or to others.

Once the governing instrument and trustee's statement have been filed, they need not be filed again with later tax returns, provided the later returns contain a statement showing where and when those documents were filed. However, if the instrument is amended in any way after a copy has been filed, a copy of the amendment must be filed with the return for the taxable year in which the amendment was made, and the trustee must also file a statement indicating the effect, if any, of such amendment on the extent to which the income of the trust is taxable to the trust, the beneficiaries, the grantor, or others.

If the trust is a "grantor trust," any part of the income of the trust which is taxable to the grantor, spouse, or others will not be reported on the Form 1041. Such income and the deductions and credits applied to it must be shown in a separate statement attached to Form 1041. The name, identifying number, and address of the person to whom the income is taxable must be included in this separate statement. Also, the name of that person to whom the income is taxable must be reported in parentheses following the name of the trust in the name block at the top of Form 1041.

As for the payment of the tax, there are no provisions for installment payments, so the tax must be paid in full with the return.

The return is due to be filed by the 15th day of the fourth month following the close of the trust's taxable year, and it will be filed with the Internal Revenue Service Center for the state where the trustee resides or has his principal place of business.

CHOOSING THE BEST TAX YEAR

Since the trustee has the option of adopting any fiscal year he wishes for the filing of the trust's tax returns, it would be well for him to give this some thought soon after taking office.

One consideration might be which time of the year it would be most convenient to close the books and prepare statements and tax returns, but a more important consideration is the saving of taxes.

Very often it is best to close the books for the first time at some date short of a full twelve-month period in order to reduce the amount of income (with the resulting lower tax bracket) to be reported on the first tax return.

Also, if all or a part of the trust income is to be taxed to a beneficiary rather than to the trust, the effect on the beneficiary's income tax should be considered. The beneficiary must include such income on his individual return for his year within which, or with which, the trust's fiscal year ends, the same as for a partner and his partnership. Therefore, if, for example, a beneficiary is on a calendar year and the trust on a January 31 fiscal year, the beneficiary will get almost a year's delay in paying taxes on the trust income—not possible if the trust was also on a December 31 year.

The trustee should look ahead, giving thought to the trust and to the beneficiaries, the relative tax brackets of each, and so on, and try to decide on the tax year which will likely result in the greatest tax saving.

As for termination, a trust normally terminates according to the terms of the trust instrument which created it, or sometimes as required by state law. However, such an event does not necessarily terminate the trust for tax purposes, since a reasonable time is allowed for the orderly distribution of assets, so this might make it possible to spread some income into one additional tax year, with the probable resulting saving of taxes.

HOW TRUSTS ARE TAXED

Generally, the income earned by a trust during the period of its administration is taxable only once, either to the trust itself or to the beneficiaries, or in part to each. The disposition of the income, as directed by the trust instrument, governs its taxability.

If the income is to be accumulated by the trust rather than being distributed to beneficiaries, the trust must pay the tax on this income. If the income is required by the instrument to be turned over to certain beneficiaries, the trust will not have to pay the tax on it, but the recipients must include such income in their individual tax returns and pay the tax. If a portion of the income is retained by the trust and a portion is distributed, the trust is taxable on the retained portion and the distributees on the portions they receive.

Therefore, a Fiduciary Income Tax Return is, in effect, a cross between an individual income tax return and a partnership income tax return.

If all the income is taxable to the trust, it is taxable very much like an individual's income—a personal exemption is allowed and the tax rate schedule for a married person filing a separate return is used.

If all the income is distributable to others, the Form 1041 becomes merely an information return showing the names of the various distributees and the amounts of the several kinds of income (ordinary income, capital gains, dividend income, and others) which each received. The distributees pick up these figures from the trust return in preparing their individual returns, just as the members of a partnership obtain their income figures from the partnership tax return.

In those cases where only a part of the income is distributed, the trust must pay tax on the retained portion; the distributed portion is shown as being taxable to the recipients—the return is both an income tax return and an information return at the same time.

The tax return allocation of the trust's income is accomplished by showing any proper distributions to beneficiaries as a *deduction* from the net income for the period, previously detailed on the form. The balance remaining, if any, is taxable to the trust; a distribution schedule is provided for giving the names of recipients and other details of the deduction claimed.

Although the income taxable to a trust is subject to similar exemptions and rates as that of an individual, there are several basic differences —there is no such concept as "adjusted gross income"; there is no deduction for dependents; the percentage limitation on charitable contributions does not apply; there is no self-employment tax; no declaration of estimated tax is necessary; income-averaging is not permitted; and others.

TO WHOM TRUST INCOME IS TAXED

Determination of the proper amount of the distributions to beneficiaries to be claimed as a deduction on the trust tax return, and, therefore, to whom the income shall be taxed, is subject to an extremely complicated set of rules.

This is treated fully in the following chapter but, for the present, the amount of income passed to the beneficiaries and taxable to them is not always simply the amount actually distributed to them. There is a limitation known as "distributable net income," so the actual taxability of trust income must be worked out in accordance with all the tax rules and limitations when the return is being prepared.

THE CONDUIT PRINCIPLE

But once the *amount* of the distribution taxable to a beneficiary is worked out, the *character* of that amount must be determined.

If the distributable net income includes various kinds of income subject to special tax treatment, such as tax-exempt interest, dividends, and others, it is necessary to determine how much of each type of income was distributed to each beneficiary.

A trust is considered as a "conduit" through which income is channeled to the beneficiaries, but without changing the nature of the income; that is, the income retains the same income tax status in the hands of the beneficiaries that it had in the hands of the fiduciary. The recipients of the distributions need to know the character of these amounts in order to report them properly on their income tax returns; the trustee needs the same information about any portion of the income retained by the trust.

To make this determination, each item of *gross* income being distributed is first reduced to *net*. Any deduction directly allocable to a particular class of gross income should be deducted from that class; unallocable deductions may be applied against any other income which was included in figuring distributable net income.

Each item of the *net* income is then apportioned among the beneficiaries on a simple proportion basis, and the trustee will, of course, give each beneficiary a Schedule K-1 showing the income tax status of various distributions.

TAX SAVINGS THROUGH USING TRUSTS

A number of possibilities for saving taxes through the use of trusts have been mentioned earlier throughout this book, and they might be summarized as follows.

The fact that a "block" of taxable income can be spread among several different taxable entities (the trust itself and possibly several different beneficiaries) makes it obvious that a tax saving will result. Each segment of the income will be taxed in a lower bracket than if taxed as a single block (unless a beneficiary already has other income and is in a higher bracket), and each entity may use its own personal exemption. Further, if the grantor had not created a trust, the entire income from the property would be taxed to him along with any other income he might have and be taxed in an even higher bracket; placing *any* income-producing property in a trust almost always saves *some* income tax.

There can be an estate tax saving also, in spite of the 1976 law, because a trust can provide a vehicle for by-passing a second estate. Any time property can be made to by-pass an estate there is certain to be a (possibly very large) saving in estate taxes.

Before the enactment of the Tax Reform Act of 1976, the estate tax savings were much greater, because property placed in trust was no longer a part of the grantor's estate (unless contemplation of death was ruled), and effectively by-passed that estate. Now, however, there is added to a decedent's remaining property any that he gave away, either outright or in trust, for purposes of the unified estate and gift tax. But although the effectiveness of trusts as an estate tax saving tool has been lessened somewhat, trusts still have the same advantages otherwise as before.

As for gift taxes, there could be some saving here too, because a trust is a separate entity and the $3,000 annual gift tax exclusion can apply to gifts in trust.

In addition to the tax savings, another saving can result from the decrease in estate fees, commissions, and administrative expenses when property placed in trust by-passes a probate estate.

THE PERSONAL EXEMPTION

As with an individual, a trust may deduct a personal exemption in arriving at its taxable income, but the amount is less. If the trust is required to distribute all of its income currently its exemption is $300. All other trusts are allowed a personal exemption deduction of $100.

The tax benefit of the exemption is lost, however, if the trust does not have retained income at least equal to the amount of the exemption. A beneficiary may not claim the exemption allowable to the trust even though the trust has lost the tax benefit of the deduction.

TAX RATES FOR TRUSTS

The net taxable income remaining taxable to the trust itself is taxed at the following rates:

If the taxable income is:	The tax is:
Not over $500	14% of the taxable income.
Over $500 but not over $1,000	$70, plus 15% of excess over $500.
Over $1,000 but not over $1,500	$145, plus 16% of excess over $1,000.
Over $1,500 but not over $2,000	$225, plus 17% of excess over $1,500.
Over $2,000 but not over $4,000	$310, plus 19% of excess over $2,000.
Over $4,000 but not over $6,000	$690, plus 22% of excess over $4,000.
Over $6,000 but not over $8,000	$1,130, plus 25% of excess over $6,000.
Over $8,000 but not over $10,000	$1,630, plus 28% of excess over $8,000.
Over $10,000 but not over $12,000	$2,190, plus 32% of excess over $10,000.
Over $12,000 but not over $14,000	$2,830, plus 36% of excess over $12,000.
Over $14,000 but not over $16,000	$3,550, plus 39% of excess over $14,000.
Over $16,000 but not over $18,000	$4,330, plus 42% of excess over $16,000.
Over $18,000 but not over $20,000	$5,170, plus 45% of excess over $18,000.
Over $20,000 but not over $22,000	$6,070, plus 48% of excess over $20,000.
Over $22,000 but not over $26,000	$7,030, plus 50% of excess over $22,000.
Over $26,000 but not over $32,000	$9,030, plus 53% of excess over $26,000.
Over $32,000 but not over $38,000	$12,210, plus 55% of excess over $32,000.
Over $38,000 but not over $44,000	$15,510, plus 58% of excess over $38,000.
Over $44,000 but not over $50,000	$18,990, plus 60% of excess over $44,000.
Over $50,000 but not over $60,000	$22,590, plus 62% of excess over $50,000.
Over $60,000 but not over $70,000	$28,790, plus 64% of excess over $60,000.
Over $70,000 but not over $80,000	$35,190, plus 66% of excess over $70,000.
Over $80,000 but not over $90,000	$41,790, plus 68% of excess over $80,000.
Over $90,000 but not over $100,000	$48,590, plus 69% of excess over $90,000.
Over $100,000	$55,490, plus 70% of excess over $100,000.

Trusts may not use the tables for taxable incomes under $20,000 as individuals do.

ALTERNATIVE TAX AND MINIMUM TAX

A trust can take advantage of the alternative tax computation, which is similar to that used by individuals. If the trust has capital gains taxable to it rather than to a beneficiary and if its taxable income is more than $26,000, the alternative tax computation schedule on the Schedule D for Form 1041 should be completed for a possible reduction in tax.

As for the minimum tax, a trust can be subject to this in the same way as a corporation. Tax preference items must first be apportioned between the trust and the beneficiaries on the basis of the income allocable to each, and if the trust's portion of these items is more than $30,000 ($10,000 after December 31, 1975) a Form 4626, Computation of Minimum Tax, should be completed and attached to the Form 1041.

Tax preference items distributed to beneficiaries should be entered on the Schedule K-1 given to each beneficiary; there is a space on the schedule for showing these.

CREDITS AGAINST THE TAX

In general, a trust gets the same credits against its tax as an individual. These credits are as follows:

Foreign Tax Credit: The trustee may elect to claim credit for income taxes paid to a foreign country or a possession of the United States. This credit is allowable only to the extent that these taxes are not allocable to the beneficiaries, and a Form 1116 should be filed if the credit is claimed.

Investment Credit: The rules for computing the investment credit are the same as for any other taxpayer, and a Form 3468 should be attached showing this computation, but including only the portion allocable to the trust on the basis of the trust income apportioned to the trust. Another schedule showing each beneficiary's share should be attached, and the beneficiary should be notified of this. Recapture of an earlier year's investment credit must also be computed by a trust if property is disposed of before the life-years category used in computing the investment credit;

the rules are the same as for other taxpayers and the same form, Form 4255, must be completed and attached.

Work Incentive Credit: A trust engaged in a trade or business is allowed a credit for its share (again on an income allocation basis) of certain salaries and wages of employees certified as being under a work incentive program. A Form 4874 should be completed for the trust's portion of this credit. If a recapture of this credit becomes necessary, the recapture amount is shown on the Form 1041 and the computation should be shown on an attached schedule.

Credit on Covenant Bond Interest: The trust's share of the credit for tax paid at the source on tax-free covenant bond interest is claimed directly on the Form 1041.

Credit for Tax on Certain Fuels: A credit may be claimed for the tax on gasoline or lubricating oil used for nonhighway purposes and others described on Form 4136, which should be attached to Form 1041.

Credit from Regulated Investment Companies: A trust may also be entitled to a credit from regulated investment companies; if so, the credit should be supported by a Form 2439.

7

DETERMINING FIGURES FOR THE TRUST TAX RETURN

At first glance, a fiduciary income tax return might seem to be rather simple and easy to prepare. But there are many hidden complexities which a practitioner must be aware of and understand before he can prepare the return correctly.

Some trusts, of course, might contain few, if any, of these complexities, and preparation of the tax return would be easy. Most trusts, however, do present some tax problems, and a return preparer can very easily become lost in a maze on account of these problems and end up preparing a return which is not at all correct.

Therefore, an understanding of the various possible tax problems is essential, and it is strongly recommended that before actually preparing a return the practitioner go through a series of steps for determining the correct disposition of each of these problems and for arriving at all the figures which will be needed in the actual completion of the return.

Each of these steps is described in this chapter; if each is followed, everything needed for the preparation of the return itself will be readily available.

THE STARTING POINT—
FIDUCIARY ACCOUNTING INCOME

The starting point in arriving at a trust's taxable income is always the fiduciary accounting income, assuming that the trust books have been kept correctly in accordance with whatever the provisions of the trust instrument and local law have dictated.

As mentioned earlier, fiduciary accounting income might or might not be the same as taxable income, but most often the two are very different. For example, fiduciary accounting income might not include capital gains and losses, but taxable income would include them; it might include tax-exempt income, taxable income does not; certain expenses might not have been deducted from fiduciary accounting income, but they may be deducted for taxable income; and others.

Each adjustment necessary to bring fiduciary accounting income down to taxable income will be described later but, first, it might be well to become familiar with some of the tax concepts peculiar to trust taxation and with the treatment of a number of specific income and deduction simple and complex trusts items which are likely to cause difficulty in trust taxation.

SIMPLE AND COMPLEX TRUSTS

The tax laws classify all trusts as either "simple" or "complex" trusts. Code Section 651 defines a simple trust as one which meets the following requirements for the taxable year:

(1) the governing instrument provides that all trust income be distributed currently;
(2) the governing instrument does not provide for transfers for charitable purposes; and
(3) the trust makes no distribution except of current income.

All other trusts—those which do not qualify as simple trusts—are complex trusts. The latter category would include trusts in which income may be accumulated and those in which principal is actually distributed.

This classification of trusts seems to be occasioned mainly by the exigencies of draftsmanship. It has apparently been found more convienient to cast the rules for trusts that are required to pay out all their income but do not distribute principal (simple trusts) separately from the more complicated rules for trusts governed by additional provisions with respect to distributions of principal and income (complex trusts). The label is accordingly significant in ascertaining the appropriate tax rules, but for fiduciary purposes this classification is not of any very great importance.

A trust might change its nature from year to year. For example, if a simple trust should distribute any corpus during the year, whether pursuant to a power of invasion or incidental to the termination of the trust, the trust becomes complex for that year. (A simple trust always becomes complex in the year of termination because principal is distributed on termination.)

Although a trust instrument requires a simple trust to distribute all its current income currently, the trustee may actually hold back in a particular year without spoiling the "simple" character of the trust. Furthermore, the trust itself will still be allowed to claim as a deduction the amount *required* to be distributed, to the extent that it consists of taxable income of the trust. It does not matter that the actual distribution is delayed beyond the end of the taxable year.

Unfortunately for the beneficiaries of simple trusts, Section 652 (c) requires that they include in taxable income the amounts required to be distributed to them during the taxable year, whether or not the distribution actually took place.

A provision requiring the allocation of all capital gains to corpus will not keep a trust from being a simple trust. The determination of what is "income" depends on the terms of the governing instrument and applicable local law. Thus, if capital gains are allocable to corpus, then even though they will be taxed to the trust, they are not income for distribution purposes.

CURRENTLY DISTRIBUTABLE INCOME

The next concept—a very important one—with which it is necessary to become familiar has to do with determining the proper amount to be used as a deduction for distributions to beneficiaries.

The basic concept underlying income taxation of trusts is that all taxable income shall be taxed only once—either to the trust or to the beneficiaries, or in part to each. Double taxation is avoided by treating the trust as a conduit and allowing it to deduct distributions to beneficiaries who, in turn, must include these distributions in their own taxable income. It is possible, and not unusual, for this deduction to eliminate entirely the trust's taxable income and leave the trust with no tax to pay.

Basically, the deduction is the lower of:
1. income required to be distributed currently, explained in this section; or,
2. the trust's distributable net income, explained in the following section.

Currently distributable income is any portion of the trust's income which is required to be distributed currently to the beneficiaries, *and* any other amounts paid, credited, or required to be distributed for the tax year.

As for income required to be distributed, neither the fact that the income is of such a nature as to make its distribution difficult, nor that it cannot be exactly ascertained until after the close of the year affects its nature as currently distributable income. It does not have to have been actually distributed within the tax year to qualify as currently distributable income; it qualifies even though it is not distributed until after the end of the year.

But as for "other amounts paid or credited," these are included as currently distributable income only if they were actually distributed during the year, or at least made available upon demand. There are cases where the trustee is not authorized to distribute all of the current income but may make distributions out of corpus; such distributions, if properly paid or credited, will qualify as currently distributable income to the extent that they are actually paid out of income—that is, to the extent of current income less any portion required to be distributed.

Currently distributable income means, generally, net fiduciary accounting income. The charges to income are usually the ordinary expense deductions familiar to accountants, but it is possible for the trust instrument or state law to redefine some of these, so the accountant must be sure to know the correct definition of "charges" applicable to his particular case.

Currently distributable income can never include amounts which did not enter into taxable gross income in the first place—tax-exempt interest, for example. And the expenses attributable to tax-exempt income must also be excluded in determining the currently distributable income.

DISTRIBUTABLE NET INCOME CONCEPT

The deduction for currently distributable income is subject to a ceiling known as "distributable net income" (DNI). This ceiling not only limits the trust's deduction but also the amounts the beneficiaries must include in their gross income.

The trust's *taxable* income, before any deduction for distributions, is the starting point in computing distributable net income. To this figure:

1. Add back the personal exemption.
2. Add back the dividend exclusion, if any.

3. Add back the 50 percent long-term capital gain deduction.
4. Deduct gross capital gains allocable to corpus. (Leave only that portion of net capital gains paid, credited, or required to be distributed.)
5. Add back tax-exempt interest (unless allocable to charitable contributions) less expenses applicable to such income.

The result is the distributable net income of the trust for the year.

Distributable net income, therefore, often becomes very much the same as fiduciary accounting income, and it may seem foolish to start with fiduciary accounting income, then work it down to taxable income, then work that back up to distributable net income, but it is strongly recommended that this procedure be followed exactly—there is no other way of determining correctly, in all cases, the amount of DNI.

Distributions in excess of DNI are not deductible by the trust and are not taxable to the beneficiaries. Distributions of less than DNI are deductible to that extent, taxable to the beneficiaries in like amount, and the undistributed balance is taxed to the trust. In all cases where DNI includes tax-exempt income, the distributions deduction is limited to DNI as reduced by the net tax exempt income.

TAX-EXEMPT INCOME

Trusts very often have part of their assets in bonds which produce tax-exempt income. Such income is, of course, fiduciary accounting income even though it is not taxable, so this is one of the adjustments often required to bring fiduciary accounting income down to taxable income, then back to DNI.

Tax-exempt income must be taken into account in determining the actual deduction for distributions because, as mentioned earlier, the deduction is limited to DNI *minus* any items not included in gross taxable income in the first place.

Under the Section 265 rule governing all taxpayers, the expenses of a trust (including interest, trustee's fee, and others) which are attributable to the production of tax-exempt income are not deductible. The allocation of these expenses is one of the first steps to be taken before preparing the tax return, as explained in a following section.

TREATMENT OF ADMINISTRATIVE EXPENSES

A trust instrument might specify that administrative expenses shall be considered a charge against income or against corpus or in part against each. This governs the treatment of these expenses for fiduciary accounting purposes—only those specified as being allocable to income will reduce the trust's income.

But even though all or a part of adminstrative expenses are charged to corpus for fiduciary accounting purposes, this does not affect their deductibility for tax purposes, and this is another of the adjustments required in arriving at the trust's taxable income.

However, if there is tax-exempt income, a part of the administrative expenses will have to be allocated to that income and not be deductible after all.

TREATMENT OF DEPRECIATION

The accounting treatment of depreciation depends on the trust instrument. If the instrument mentions depreciation as an expense, a reserve should be set up with a corresponding charge against income, just as with any commercial business. If it says that no depreciation is to be charged against income the trust must not set up a reserve for depreciation and fiduciary accounting income will not be reduced by depreciation. If the instrument is silent regarding depreciation, local law will govern.

But depreciation is, of course, deductible for tax purposes in any case. If it has already been provided for in the accounts no adjustment is necessary. If not, the proper amount must be computed and used in adjusting fiduciary accounting income to taxable income.

Depreciation must be apportioned between the beneficiaries and the trust in proportion to the share of net fiduciary accounting income allocated to each, including any charitable beneficiaries. Thus, in a simple trust all of the depreciation goes to the beneficiaries, since they get all the income. In a complex trust a portion of the depreciation might stay with the trust and be a tax deduction on the trust tax return.

TREATMENT OF CAPITAL GAINS AND LOSSES

The trust instrument will govern whether capital gains and losses shall be allocated to the trust corpus or to fiduciary accounting income. But, again, this does not control for tax purposes, and these gains and losses must be reported on the tax return even though, for fiduciary accounting purposes, they become a part of corpus.

Capital gains and losses are generally taken into account in computing taxable income just as if the trust were an individual, and a Schedule D, Form 1041, is used to report all such transactions.

Any part of the net gain that is properly paid, credited, or required to be distributed during the year to a beneficiary is deductible by the fiduciary as a distribution and is taxable to the beneficiary to the extent of distributable net income, even if the gain is allocated to corpus, and the tax allocation between the trust and its beneficiaries is shown on the Schedule D. If there are several beneficiaries, the proportion of the net gains going to each will be shown on the Schedule K-1 given to each; and it will be shown as either long-term or short-term capital gain income so that the beneficiary may report it properly on his tax return (the conduit principle). It will be shown on his Schedule D, Form 1040.

Undistributed net long-term capital gain, taxable to the trust, is subject to the usual fifty percent reduction in arriving at taxable income, and the alternative tax computation is used when taxable income includes net long-term capital gains and exceeds $26,000.

A net capital loss, however, is deductible only by the trust, not by a beneficiary, and the rules for individuals apply—the loss deduction is limited to $1,000 per year (increased for years beginning after December 31, 1976), any unused loss may be carried forward, and so forth.

Any unused capital loss carryover remaining at the time of termination of the trust may be used by the distributees as a capital loss carryover on their individual returns. (See Chapter 9, Termination of Trusts.)

Gains and losses from the sale or exchange of property other than capital assets are reported separately on the trust tax return and must be supported by a Form 4797.

CONTRIBUTIONS TO CHARITIES

A trust's contributions to charities are distributions rather than expenses, but for tax purposes they are handled in a different way from distributions to individuals.

Contributions are shown on the tax return as a *deduction,* and the trust may take this deduction for amounts which, under the terms of the trust instrument, are paid or permanently set aside for charitable, religious, educational, or similar purposes. Unlike the charitable deduction allowed individuals, there is no percentage limitation on the amount that can be deducted.

Under Section 642 (c) income actually distributed to charities during the year is currently deductible. In addition, trusts created on or before

October 9, 1969 can in many cases deduct income permanently set aside for charities during the year. Trustees can also elect to deduct for a given taxable year contributions paid before the close of the following year.

To be deductible, the contributions must be made from the *gross* income of the trust. No deduction is allowed for a contribution out of the trust principal. However, a contribution from income that is allocable to corpus, such as capital gains, will qualify for the deduction, since such income is included in the gross taxable income of the trust.

When a trust has both taxable and tax-exempt income, the contribution deduction is allowed only for the portion considered as coming from the gross taxable income. This is computed on a simple proportion basis—the proportion which the gross taxable income bears to the total income.

An adjustment must also be made when a part or all of the contribution is made out of long-term capital gains. The proportionate part of the contribution coming from long-term capital gains is computed and this figure is reduced by fifty percent; this, plus the portion of contributions coming from ordinary income, is the amount of the allowable contribution deduction.

THE DIVIDEND EXCLUSION

The $100 dividend exclusion is allowed to a trust, but it is treated as a deduction on the fiduciary income tax return rather than as an income exclusion.

The trust is entitled to this deduction only on the dividends not allocated to beneficiaries. The total dividends received will be shown as gross income on the tax return, but if any part of these were included in distributions to beneficiaries the trustee may then deduct only a *proportionate* part of the $100, depending on the proportion of dividends retained by the trust.

This proration does not affect the beneficiary. He reports the dividends received from the trust on his individual return and claims the proper dividend exclusion up to the full $100.

THE PERSONAL EXEMPTION

Generally, a simple trust gets a personal exemption deduction of $300, a complex trust gets $100.

But, to state the rule more accurately, a trust required to distribute all of its income currently gets a deduction of $300 even in a year when it distributes corpus, or amounts to charity, and therefore is not a "simple trust." All other trusts are allowed a deduction of $100.

Personal exemptions are omitted in computing the distributable net income of the trust.

The personal exemption is not allowed in the year of termination of the trust because in the year of final distribution of assets all income of the trust must be entered as distributed to beneficiaries without deduction for the personal exemption.

ALLOCATIONS REQUIRED

With the foregoing sections about the basic rules and peculiarities of trust taxation in mind, it would be well at this point to study the exact step-by-step procedures for determining all of the figures needed in preparing a trust's tax return.

There is one preliminary step which must be taken first, however. This consists of making several allocations which are required in many cases.

First, if the trust had any tax-exempt income, the trust expenses must be allocated between taxable income and the tax-exempt income, because expenses attributable to tax-exempt income are not deductible. In making this allocation all deductible items *directly* attributable to one class of income are first allocated to that class, for example, rental property repairs and expenses are allocated to gross rents; indirect expenses such as the trustee's commission, safe rentals, state income and property taxes and others are allocated, on a proportionate basis, to the various gross income items which will be included in computing distributable net income. (Regulations Section 1.652 (b)-3(b) specifically precludes the allocation of any indirect expense to an item excluded from the computation of distributable net income, such as capital gains credited to corpus.)

Next, if there is both tax-exempt income and a charitable distribution, the amount of the charitable distribution attributable to the tax-exempt income must be determined. Unless the governing instrument makes a different allocation, the contribution considered as coming from gross taxable income bears the same proportion to the total contribution as the total taxable gross income bears to the total income including tax-exempt items.

Finally, depreciation must be apportioned between each beneficiary, including any charitable beneficiaries, and the trust in proportion to the share of net fiduciary accounting income allocated to each.

FIVE STEPS IN ARRIVING
AT TAXABLE INCOME

After making the necessary allocations, the following steps should be taken:

1. Start with
   FIDUCIARY ACCOUNTING INCOME

2. Make all necessary adjustments to arrive at
   TAXABLE INCOME BEFORE DISTRIBUTIONS DEDUCTON

3. Adjust this figure back to
   DISTRIBUTABLE NET INCOME

4. Eliminate tax-exempt income to arrive at
   DISTRIBUTIONS DEDUCTION

5. Go back to Taxable Income Before Distributions Deduction, Step 2, and subtract the Distributions Deduction, to arrive at
   TAXABLE INCOME OF THE TRUST

Each of these steps is explained more fully in the following sections.

Again, this may seem a rather circuitous route to have to follow, but there is no other way in which all the necessary figures can be arrived at correctly.

TAXABLE INCOME BEFORE THE
DISTRIBUTIONS DEDUCTION

Taxable Income Before the Distributions Deduction is Fiduciary Accounting Income adjusted for any items which must be included (or excluded) for tax purposes which have not been considered in arriving at Fiduciary Accounting Income in the first place. These possible adjustments are:

Subtract: Administration expenses allocated to corpus in the trust books.

Add: Capital gains belonging to corpus.

Subtract: Capital losses belonging to corpus.

Subtract: The fifty percent deduction for net long-term capital gains, if any.

Subtract: Tax-exempt income reduced by the amount of expenses allocated to this income.

Add: Any taxable income which was assigned to corpus, such as a pension payment.

Subtract: Charitable contributions made from income (gross, without reduction for portion made from exempt income).

Add: The portion of charitable contributions attributable to tax-exempt income.

Subtract: Depreciation allocated to the trust.

Subtract: The dividend exclusion of $100 (adjustment will be made later for any portion not excludible by the trust).

Subtract: The personal exemption of $300 for a simple trust or $100 for a complex trust.

There could possibly be some other, more unusual, transactions requiring adjustment, but those adjustments listed above are generally all that are necessary to bring Fiduciary Accounting Income down to Taxable Income Before the Distributions Deduction.

DISTRIBUTABLE NET INCOME

Starting with Taxable Income Before the Distributions Deduction, as determined above, the following steps are taken to arrive at Distributable Net Income.

Add: The personal exemption.

Add: The $100 dividend exclusion.

Add: The fifty percent net long-term capital gain deduction.

Subtract: Capital gains belonging to corpus.

Add: Capital losses belonging to corpus.

Add: Tax-exempt income net of expenses allocated to this income.

Subtract: Undeductible portion of contributions due to tax-exempt income.

Subtract: Extraordinary income items, such as a pension payment.

The resulting Distributable Net Income is, again, the maximum amount which can be claimed as a distributions deduction by the trust.

DISTRIBUTIONS DEDUCTION

The amount of the Distributions Deduction is arrived at by simply subtracting from Distributable Net Income the amount of tax-exempt income net of any expenses allocated to this income.

However, it must be remembered that the actual deduction is limited to actual distributions, so the proper amount to use is sometimes less than the figure determined here. Therefore, a computation of the actual distributions to beneficiaries less any exempt income included in these distributions must be made; if this is less than the Distributions Deduction determined above, the lower figure is the one which must be used on the tax return.

TAXABLE INCOME OF THE TRUST

The net Taxable Income of the Trust will be computed by going back to Taxable Income Before the Distributions Deduction, determined above, and subtracting from this figure the proper Distributions Deduction figure described in the preceding section.

One other adjustment may be necessary. If a portion of the trust's dividends were distributed, a proportionate part of the $100 dividend exclusion must be added back at this point. In the case of a simple trust all of the dividends will have been distributed, so the full $100 will be added in arriving at the Taxable Income of the Trust.

WORKSHEET FOR DETERMINING ALL FIGURES

All of the above steps taken in determining the figures needed for the preparation of a trust's tax return can be summarized into a worksheet which will serve for any trust, simple or complex.

By following this worksheet, filling in only those blanks necessary for the particular trust, every figure needed will be readily available and the actual preparation of the tax return itself becomes a simple matter. This worksheet is given on page 117.

WORKSHEET FOR TRUST TAX RETURN

Line
1 ALLOCATIONS REQUIRED:
2   Expenses Attributable to Taxable Income . . . . $_____
3   Expenses Attributable to Exempt Income . . . . $_____
4   Charitable Deduction Attributable to Taxable Income . . . . $_____
5   Charitable Deduction Attributable to Exempt Income . . . . $_____
6   Depreciation Apportioned on Basis of Fiduciary
7   Accounting Income Allocated to Each:
8   Charity . . . . $_____
9   Beneficiary A . . . . $_____
10   Beneficiary B . . . . $_____
11   Trust . . . . $_____
12 FIDUCIARY ACCOUNTING INCOME . . . . $_____
13   —Administration Expenses Allocated to Corpus . . . . (_____)
14   +Capital Gains Belonging to Corpus . . . . _____
15   —Capital Losses Belonging to Corpus . . . . (_____)
16   —Capital Gain Deduction of 50% . . . . (_____)
17   —Tax-Exempt Income, Net of Allocated Expenses . . . . (_____)
18   +Taxable Income Assigned to Corpus (Such as Pension Payment) . _____
19   —Charitable Contributions Made From Income . . . . (_____)
20   +Portion of Contributions Attributable to Exempt Income . . . . _____
21   —Depreciation Allocated to the Trust . . . . (_____)
22   —Dividend Exclusion of $100 . . . . (_____)
23   —The Personal Exemption ($100 or $300) . . . . (_____)
24 = TAXABLE INCOME BEFORE DISTRIBUTIONS DEDUCTION . . . . . . $_____
25   +The Personal Exemption . . . . _____
26   +Dividend Exclusion of $100 . . . . _____
27   +Capital Gain Deduction of 50% . . . . _____
28   —Capital Gains Belonging to Corpus . . . . (_____)
29   +Capital Losses Belonging to Corpus . . . . _____
30   +Tax-Exempt Income, Net of Allocated Expenses . . . . _____
31   —Undeductible Portion of Contributions Due to Exempt Income . . . (_____)
32   —Extraordinary Income Items (Such as Pension Payments) . . . . (_____)
33 = DISTRIBUTABLE NET INCOME . . . . $_____
34   —Tax-Exempt Income, Net of Allocated Expenses and the Portion
         of Contributions Attributable to Exempt Income . . . . (_____)
35 = DISTRIBUTIONS DEDUCTION . . . . $_____
      (The Distributions Deduction is limited, however, to actual
      distributions, less exempt income included in the distributions)
36 TAXABLE INCOME BEFORE DISTRIBUTIONS DEDUCTION (Above) $_____
37   —Distribution Deduction   (_____)
38   +Portion of Dividend Exclusion Applicable to Distributions . . . . _____
39 = TAXABLE INCOME OF THE TRUST . . . . $_____

EXAMPLE OF USE OF WORKSHEET

To illustrate the use of the worksheet, assume that a simple trust had the following items of income and expense for the year 1977: *

Rents	$25,000.00*
Dividends of Domestic Corporations	50,000.00*
Tax-Exempt Interest on Bonds	25,000.00*
Long-term Capital Gains	15,000.00
Expenses Attributable to Rents	5,000.00*
Trustee's Commissions	
Allocable to Corpus	1,300.00
Trustee's Commissions	
Allocable to Income	2,600.00*
Depreciation	5,000.00

Under the terms of the trust **instrument**, all of the income is to be distributed equally to the grantor's widow **and** son. Capital gains are to be allocated to corpus, and no provision for depreciation is made in the trust instrument.

Only the starred items in the above listing are income and expense for fiduciary accounting purposes, resulting in a net Fiduciary Accounting Income of $92,400, and this is the income required to be distributed currently.

The worksheet for the trust tax return will be completed as shown on page 119.

The taxable income is the net long-term capital gain less the 50% deduction, $7,500, which was not distributed to the beneficiaries because it was not a part of fiduciary accounting income, and less the trust's personal exemption of $300, or $7,200.

Next, it is necessary to **analyze** the character of the distributions so that each beneficiary will know how to report the various items on his individual tax return. Assuming that the trustee elects to allocate to rental income the expenses attributable to taxable income, $2,925, the distributions will consist of:

	Rents	Dividends	Exempt Interest	Total
Income	$25,000.00	$50,000.00	$25,000.00	$100,000.00
Rental Expenses	(5,000.00)	—	—	(5,000.00)
Trustee's Commission	(2,925.00)	—	(975.00)	(3,900.00)
Distributions	$17,075.00	$50,000.00	$24,025.00	$ 91,100.00

Each beneficiary has received one-half of each kind of net income, and this information will be needed in preparing the Schedules K-1.

After transferring all of the above information to the tax return, the applicable schedules of the return will be as shown on pages 120-122.

---

*Federal Tax Guide, 1976, published by Prentice-Hall, Inc.

ALLOCATIONS REQUIRED

Expenses Attributable to Taxable Income	$ 2,925.00
Expenses Attributable to Exempt Income	$ 975.00
(¾ and ¼ of $3,900.00 expenses excluding	
those directly attributable to rent income)	
Depreciation Apportioned on Basis of Fiduciary	
Accounting Income Allocated to:	
Widow	$ 2,500.00
Son	$ 2,500.00
Trust	-0-
(½ of the $5,000.00 to each)	

FIDUCIARY ACCOUNTING INCOME	(92,400.00)
— Administration Expenses Allocated to Corpus	(1,300.00)
+ Capital Gains Belonging to Corpus	15,000.00
— Capital Gains Deduction of 50%	(7,500.00)
— Tax-Exempt Income, Net of Allocated Expenses	(24,025.00)
— Depreciation Allocated to the Trust	-
— Dividend Exclusion	(100.00)
— The Personal Exemption	(300.00)
= TAXABLE INCOME BEFORE THE DISTRIBUTIONS DEDUCTION	$74,175.00
+The Personal Exemption	300.00
+Dividend Exclusion	100.00
+Capital Gain Deduction of 50%	7,500.00
+Capital Gains Belonging to Corpus	(15,000.00)
+Tax-Exempt Income, Net of Allocated Expenses	24,025.00
= DISTRIBUTABLE NET INCOME	$91,100.00
— Tax-Exempt Income, Net of Allocated Expenses	(24,025.00)
= DISTRIBUTION DEDUCTION	$67,075.00
TAXABLE INCOME BEFORE THE DISTRIBUTIONS DEDUCTION	$74,175.00
— Distributions Deduction	(67,075.00)
+ Dividend Exclusion Applicable to Distributions	100.00
= TAXABLE INCOME OF THE TRUST	$ 7,200.00

INCOME	1 Dividends (Enter full amount before exclusion)	1	50,000.00	
	2 Interest	2		
	3 Income from partnerships and other fiduciaries	3		
	4 Gross rents and royalties	4	25,000.00	
	5 Gross profit (loss) from trade or business	5		
	6 Net gain (loss) from capital assets (Attach Schedule D (Form 1041))	6	15,000.00	
	7 Ordinary gains and (losses) (Attach Form 4797)	7		
	8 Other income (State nature of income)	8		
	9 Total income (lines 1 to 8, inclusive)	9		90,000.00
DEDUCTIONS	10 Interest	10		
	11 Taxes	11		
	12 Fiduciary's portion of depreciation (Schedule A) and depletion. Explain depletion	12		
	13 Charitable deduction (Schedule B, line 9)	13		
	14 Other deductions (Itemize) Rent Expenses 5,000.00, Trustee's Commission 2,925.00	14	7,925.00	
	15 Total (lines 10 to 14, inclusive)	15		7,925.00
	16 Line 9 minus line 15 (Complex trusts and estates enter this amount in Schedule C, line 1 also)	16		82,075.00
	17 Deduction for distributions to beneficiaries	17	67,075.00	
	18 Adjustment of dividend exclusion	18		
	19 Federal estate tax attributable to income in respect of a decedent (Fiduciary's share)	19		
	20 Long-term capital gain deduction. Enter 50% of Schedule D (Form 1041) line 17e	20	7,500.00	
	21 Exemption (If final return, see General Instruction M.)	21	300.00	
	22 Total (lines 17 to 21, inclusive)	22		74,875.00
	23 Taxable income of fiduciary (line 16 minus line 22)	23		7,200.00

Form 1041   Page 2

Schedule A.—DEPRECIATION—(See the Instructions for Schedule A for information on the depreciation methods.)

a. Group and guideline class or description of property	b. Date acquired	c. Cost or other basis	d. Depreciation allowed or allowable in prior years	e. Method of computing depreciation	f. Life or rate	g. Depreciation for this year
1 Total additional first-year depreciation—estates only (do not include in items below)						
2 Depreciation from Form 4832						
3 Depreciation from Form 5006						
4 Other depreciation: Rental Property						5,000.00
5 Totals						5,000.00
6 Less amount of depreciation claimed elsewhere on return						
7 Balance (line 5 minus line 6)						5,000.00
8 Fiduciary's portion of line 7. Enter here and on page 1, line 12						-0-

Schedule C.—DISTRIBUTABLE NET INCOME AND DISTRIBUTIONS DEDUCTION

1 Enter amount from page 1, line 16	1	82,075.00
2 Add: a Tax-exempt interest (as adjusted)	2a	24,025.00
b Net gain shown on Schedule D (Form 1041) line 16, column 1. If net loss, enter zero	b	-
c Schedule B, lines 4 and 7	c	-
d Short-term capital gain included on Schedule B, line 1	d	-
e If amount on page 1, line 6, is a loss, enter amount here as a positive figure	e	-
3 Total (line 1 through line 2e)	3	106,100.00
4 If amount on page 1, line 6, is a gain, enter amount here	4	15,000.00
5 Distributable net income (line 3 minus line 4)	5	91,100.00
6 Amount of income required to be distributed currently	6	92,400.00
7 Other amounts paid, credited, or otherwise required to be distributed	7	-
8 Total (lines 6 and 7)	8	92,400.00
9 Enter the total of tax-exempt income included on lines 6 and 7 (as adjusted)	9	24,025.00
10 Balance (line 8 minus line 9)	10	68,375.00
11 Enter distributable net income (line 5, above)	11	91,100.00
12 Enter the amount from line 2a, above	12	24,025.00
13 Balance (line 11 minus line 12)	13	67,075.00
14 Distributions deduction. Enter here and on page 1, line 17, the lesser of line 10 or line 13 above	14	67,075.00

(This Schedule C is given for illustrative purposes only, but it is not required to be completed for simple trusts.)

SCHEDULE D
(Form 1041)
Department of the Treasury
Internal Revenue Service

Capital Gains and Losses

Name of estate or trust

Employer identification number

Part I	**Short-term Capital Gains and Losses—Assets Held Not More Than 6 Months**					
	a. Kind of property and description (Example, 100 shares of "Z" Co.)	**b.** Date acquired (mo., day, yr.)	**c.** Date sold (mo., day, yr.)	**d.** Gross sales price	**e.** Cost or other basis, as adjusted, and expense of sale	**f.** Gain or (loss) (d less e)
1						
2	Enter net short-term gain or (loss) from partnerships and other fiduciaries				2	
3	Net gain or (loss), combine lines 1 and 2				3	
4	Short-term capital loss carryover (Attach computation)				4 (	)
5	Net short-term gain or (loss), combine lines 3 and 4. Enter here and on line 14 below				5	

Part II	**Long-term Capital Gains and Losses—Assets Held More Than 6 Months**					
6	Gains					15,000.00
7	Capital gain dividends				7	
8	Enter gain, if applicable, from Form 4797 line 4(a)(1)				8	
9	Enter net long-term gain or (loss) from partnerships and other fiduciaries				9	
10	Enter net long-term gain from small business corporations (subchapter S)				10	
11	Net gain or (loss), combine lines 6 through 10				11	
12	Long-term capital loss carryover (Attach computation)				12 (	)
13	Net long-term gain or (loss), combine lines 11 and 12. Enter here and on line 15 below				13	15,000.00

Part III	**Summary of Parts I and II**	1. Beneficiaries	2. Fiduciary	3. Total
14	Net short-term gain or (loss) from line 5, above			
15	Net long-term gain or (loss) from line 13, above		15,000.00	15,000.00
16	Total net gain or (loss)		15,000.00	15,000.00

Enter on Form 1041, page 1, line 6, the net gain shown on line 16, column 3, above. If net (loss) on line 16, column 3, above, enter as (loss) on Form 1041, page 1, line 6, the amount computed on line 18b.

Computation of Capital Gains Deduction

17	**a**	Long-term capital gain shown on line 15, column 3, above	17a	15,000.00
	b	Short-term capital loss shown on line 14, column 3, above	17b (	)
	c	Excess of line 17a over line 17b, above	17c	15,000.00
	d	Long-term capital gains taxable to beneficiaries. (Total of line 3 amounts from all separate Schedules K–1 (Form 1041))	17d	–0–
	e	Balance (line 17c minus line 17d). (Enter 50% of this amount on Form 1041, page 1, line 20)	17e	15,000.00

Computation of Capital Loss Limitation

18 Attach a computation if losses are shown on both lines 12 and 13 which are the result of a long-term capital loss carryover from years beginning before 1970, enter the amount on line 18a and note "Computation attached"; see Part IV of your retained copy of the 1975 Schedule D (Form 1041). Otherwise,

  a Enter one of the following amounts:
   i If amount on line 14, column 3 is zero or a net gain, enter 50% of amount on line 16, column 3;
   ii If amount on line 15, column 3 is zero or a net gain, enter amount on line 16, column 3; or,
   iii If amounts on line 14, column 3 and line 15, column 3 are net losses, enter amount on line 14, column 3 added to 50% of amount on line 15, column 3 . . . . **18a**

  b Enter here and enter as a (loss) on Form 1041, page 1, line 6, the smallest of:
   i The amount on line 18a;
   ii $1,000; or,
   iii Taxable income computed without regard to capital gains and losses and the deduction for exemption . . . . . **18b** ( )

Note: Enter the capital loss carryover to 1977:

	Pre 1970	Post 1969
Short-term		
Long-term		

SCHEDULE K–1
(Form 1041)
Department of the Treasury
Internal Revenue Service

Beneficiary's Share of Income, Deductions, Credits, etc.—1976

for the calendar year 1976, or fiscal year

beginning ...., 1976, ending ...., 19......

(Complete for each beneficiary—see instructions on back of Copy C and the instructions for Form 1041)

Copy A

File with
Form 1041

(a) Allocable share item	(b) Amount	(c) Form 1040 filers enter column (b) amount as indicated below
1 Dividends (amount before exclusion)	25,000.00	Schedule B, Part I, line 1
2 Short-term capital gain		Schedule D, line 2
3 Long-term capital gain		Schedule D, line 9
4 a Other taxable income (Itemize) .... Net Rents	8,537.50	
b		
c Total of lines 4a and 4b	8,537.50	
d Depreciation and depletion (See Sch. A (1041) instrs.) . . .	2,500.00	
e Amortization deductions (Itemize) (See 1041 instr. 14.)		
f		
g Total of lines 4d, 4e and 4f	2,500.00	
h Line 4c minus line 4g	6,037.50	Schedule E, Part III
5 Foreign taxes (Attach schedule)		Form 1116 or Schedule A (Form 1040), line 16
6 a Other (Itemize)...................................		Enter on applicable line of appropriate tax form
b		Enter on applicable line of appropriate tax form
Tax Preference Items: 7 Long-term capital gain		See Form 4625 Instructions
8 Depreciation (real property)		Form 4625, line 1(b) (2)
9 Depletion		Form 4625, line 1(j)
10 a Other (Itemize)................................		Enter on applicable line of Form 4625
b		Enter on applicable line of Form 4625

Name, identifying number, and address (including ZIP code) of beneficiary

Name and employer identification number of estate or trust and name and address (including ZIP code) of fiduciary

8

COMPLETING THE TRUST TAX RETURN

Completion of the trust tax return and its supporting schedules is not too difficult if the worksheet has been filled in properly; practically everything needed will appear on the worksheet, plus a simple analysis of the distributions, as illustrated in the preceding chapter.

There are a few tax rules which have not been mentioned previously, however, and there might remain some questions of exactly how to show certain items on the return, so the step-by-step completion of the tax return is covered in this chapter, as well as the additional tax rules which might come into play in certain cases.

INCOME ITEMS TO REPORT

The income items to report are, in general, exactly what would be expected, and each item is reported in full without considering whether or not any part of it may have been distributed.

The full amount of dividends before the dividend exclusion is shown; interest income is shown if it is taxable, but tax-exempt interest is ignored and does not appear on the Form 1041; the trust's share of income from partnerships and other fiduciaries is included; rental income is shown gross, with related expenses being deducted later; if there is a trade or business involved, the instructions say that the *gross profit* from the business should be shown as income with the related expenses being deducted later (and a statement must be attached showing the nature of the business, its gross profit, deductions, and net income); net capital gain or loss, before the fifty percent deduction, is shown as income, supported by a Schedule D, Form 1041; ordinary gains and losses will also be shown, supported by a Form 4797; and any other income items, such as the taxable income from a small business corporation, must also be included in the income section of the Form 1041.

EXPENSES AND OTHER DEDUCTIONS TO REPORT

Next, all proper deductions are entered. But it must be remembered at this point that any expenses which have been allocated to tax-exempt income must be eliminated—they do not appear on the return in any place.

Deductible expenses might include interest paid (except, of course, interest on a debt incurred or continued to buy or carry obligations yielding tax-exempt income); taxes such as property taxes, state income taxes, and the other deductible taxes, but excluding any federal income tax paid by the trust; depreciation, if any, allocated to the trust rather than to beneficiaries, as detailed in Schedule A of the return; the charitable deduction, supported by Schedule B; rental expenses; the expenses of a trade or business (to offset the gross business profit shown as income); investment advisory fees; the trustee's commission (again excluding any portion allocated to exempt income); and possibly others.

Also entered as deductions are the deduction for distributions to beneficiaries, previously determined and appearing on the worksheet (and supported by Schedule C of the tax return); the portion of the $100 dividend exclusion applicable to the trust's retained portion of dividends received; federal estate tax attributable to income in respect of a decedent (the fiduciary's share based on the percentage of such income not distributed); the long-term capital gain deduction, which is not simply fifty percent of the net gain previously shown as income but is fifty percent of that net long-term capital gain as reduced by any portion of *long-term* gains distributed and taxable to beneficiaries (the Schedule D has a place for making this computation); and, finally, the personal exemption permitted (but none is permitted in the trust's final year).

After entering all items of income and deductions on the Form 1041, the trust's taxable net income will be shown, and this should, of course, agree with the amount previously determined on the worksheet.

CAPITAL GAINS AND LOSSES

The rules for determination of a trust's capital gains and losses are just the same as for an individual, with one important exception as described in the following section, and the Schedule D, Form 1041, which is used for reporting each such transaction is very similar to the Schedule D used by individuals.

The *total* net gain or loss shown by the Schedule D is carried to the income section of the Form 1041, except that if there is a net loss it is subject to the same limitation on the amount of its deductibility as with an individual. The allocation of these gains and losses between the beneficiaries and the trust is also entered on the Schedule D, and this information will be needed later in completing the schedule for the distributions deduction.

The long-term capital gain deduction is computed on the Schedule D. It is done by subtracting from the net long-term capital gain the long-term capital gains taxable to beneficiaries and taking fifty percent of this figure.

As for ordinary gains and losses, the same rules as for individuals apply again. Transactions of this kind are detailed on a Form 4797 which must be attached to the Form 1041.

Non-business bad debts and losses on worthless securities are also entered on the Schedule D, as with an individual.

SPECIAL RULE FOR CERTAIN GAINS

The Tax Reform Act of 1976 added a new section to the Code, Section 644, providing a special rule for the taxation of gains on the sale of property transferred to a trust at less than fair market value. This rule is intended to cover the possible abuse where a grantor places in trust property in which he has unrealized appreciation in order to shift the payment of tax to the trust at a lower tax rate than his rate might be, and it applies to sales of property which was placed in trust after May 21, 1976.

Under this rule, where the fair market value of property placed in trust exceeds the price paid, if any, for the property by the trust (that is, where there is any bargain element in connection with the transfer), and the trust sells the property within two years of its transfer to the trust, the tax on the gain (called "includible gain") to the trust will be equal to the amount of additional tax the transferor would have paid had the gain been included in his gross income for his taxable year in which the sale occurred. In effect, such gains are treated as if the transferor had realized the gain and then transferred the net proceeds from the sale after tax to the trust.

However, where the grantor dies before the sale within the two-year period so that it would not be possible to use the rate brackets of the grantor, the provision is inapplicable and the gain is taxed at the trust's rates. To prevent circumvention of the two-year period through a short sale during such period, the law also contains a rule which extends the period to the closing of the short sale.

The character of the property (capital or ordinary) will be considered to be the same as it was in the hands of the grantor, not the trust.

The "includible gain" is the lesser of the amount of gain recognized by the trust or the amount of gain that the trust would have realized had the property been sold immediately after it was transferred to the trust. To prevent double taxation, this "includible gain" is excluded from the taxable income of the trust. Thus, the tax on the remaining income of the trust will be computed without regard to that includible gain. Also, since it is excluded from the trust's taxable income, that gain is not included in the trust's distributable net income and the gain will not be taxed to a beneficiary if it is currently distributed to him.

Moreover, since the includible gain is not in the trust's distributable net income, that gain will not be subject to the accumulation distribution rules (see Chapter 10) where the gain is first accumulated and then distributed in a later year.

CAPITAL LOSS CARRYOVER

Any capital loss which cannot be deducted currently because it exceeds the limitation on deductibility becomes a capital loss carryover.

This, also, is treated by a trust just the same as by an individual—the loss is carried to the proper section of the Schedule D for the following year and may be carried forward indefinitely until used up or absorbed by capital gains in the future.

The excess capital loss may not be passed through, currently, to beneficiaries. However, on final termination of the trust, its unused capital loss carryover may be picked up by the beneficiaries and used by them as long-term or short-term capital loss carryovers on their individual returns. The proper amount should be reported to each beneficiary on the Schedule K-1 given to him.

NET OPERATING LOSS CARRYBACK AND CARRYOVER

If a trust operates a trade or business, the business might have a net operating loss for some year. This loss is first offset against other income of the trust for that year, but any loss remaining becomes a net operating loss carryback and carryover to the trust, subject to the usual rules for handling such losses.

The loss cannot be passed through to beneficiaries currently (though they get an indirect benefit in lower taxable distributions), but it must be carried back, if elected, by the trust, to its third preceding year and so on. This carryback can affect the allowable distributions to beneficiaries in the preceding years, which might necessitate recomputation of those distributions and amending of some individual returns for the years involved. The trustee should notify each beneficiary if a situation like this occurs.

If any unused net operating loss carryover remains at the time of termination of the trust, it can then be picked up by the beneficiaries and used as explained later in the chapter on terminations.

Each beneficiary's allocable share of a net operating loss carryover should be entered as a loss on Schedule K-1 and identified as "N.O.L Carryover." However, if the last taxable year of the trust is the last year in which a net operating loss may be taken, the deduction, to the extent not absorbed in that year by the trust, is treated as an "excess deduction" (see below) and identified as "Excess Deduction on Termination."

DEPRECIATION

If depreciable property is held by the trust, the depreciation deduction is apportioned between the income beneficiaries and the trust according to the trust instrument's provisions, if any apply, otherwise on the basis of the fiduciary accounting income allocable to each. This is one of the preliminary allocations described in Chapter 7.

The usual rules for computing depreciation are followed (except that a trust may not use the additional first year depreciation allowance), and Schedule A of the Form 1041 must show the details of the depreciation claimed. The schedule must show the portion of the total depreciation allocated to the trust, and it is this amount which is used as a deduction on the Form 1041.

The portion of depreciation allocated to each beneficiary must be shown on the Schedule K-1 given to each.

THE CHARITABLE DEDUCTION

The amount actually given to a charity during the year is subject to two adjustments to arrive at the figure which can be used as a deduction. These were mentioned earlier, but, as a reminder in the preparation of the tax return, the first adjustment is the one determined in one of the preliminary allocations—the portion of the contribution attributable to tax-exempt income.

Next, an adjustment must be made when an amount is paid from long-term capital gains and the long-term capital gain deduction is allowed. First, determine the amount of the contribution coming from long-term capital gains; this bears the same proportion to the total contribution made as the total of the long-term capital gains allocated to income bears to the total income. Then, fifty percent of this amount is subtracted from the contribution. If this adjustment were not made, the same capital gain deduction would be deducted twice—once as a capital gain deduction and once as a part of the charitable deduction.

The above adjustments are shown on Schedule B of Form 1041. First, the contribution paid from the current year's fiduciary accounting income is reduced by these two adjustments; but there may then be added contributions from income allocable to corpus, specifically short-term capital gains and fifty percent of long-term capital gains of the current year; also, there may be added the total of deductible amounts paid or permanently set aside for charitable purposes to the extent that such amounts are not attributable to fiduciary accounting income of the current year or capital gains of the current year (attaching a statement to show the details). The resulting figure will be used as the charitable deduction on the Form 1041.

One other point—to enable a trustee to act after he knows the exact income for the year, he can elect to treat a current contribution as paid during the preceding tax year. The election must be made not later than the due date of the tax return for the year after the year for which the election is made, and can be revoked after that time only with Internal Revenue Service consent.

EXCESS DEDUCTIONS

If a trust has deductions in excess of its income for any tax year (except the year of its termination), these "excess deductions" are simply lost. They may not be carried backward or forward, nor may they be passed through to the beneficiaries.

But if for its final taxable year the trust has deductions (other than for the personal exemption and the charitable deduction) in excess of its gross income, these excess deductions are allowable to the beneficiaries in that year. If there are several beneficiaries, the deduction is prorated between them, based on the extent they actually share the financial burden. These should be shown on the Schedule K-1 and identified as "Excess Deductions on Termination." A beneficiary's treatment of this item is explained in the following chapter.

DEDUCTION FOR DISTRIBUTIONS

The method of determining the amount of the distributions deduction was explained earlier, and the proper amount of this deduction will be shown on the tax return worksheet, but the Schedule C, Form 1041, must be completed for a complex trust, showing in detail how the deduction was arrived at.

Most of the figures needed in completing Schedule C will appear on the worksheet, and there should be no difficulty in simply filling in the figures asked for. Without a worksheet, this schedule is often rather difficult to complete.

A simple trust is not required to complete the Schedule C because, most often, its deduction for distributions is the same as its net income in the first place.

THE 65-DAY RULE

Ordinarily, distributions are deductible by the trust and includible by the beneficiary in the year paid or payable. However, the law permits the trustee to elect to treat amounts distributed to a beneficiary within the first 65 days following the taxable year as amounts paid or credited on the last day of such taxable year. The amount eligible for election is limited to the larger of the trust income for the taxable year for which the election is made or the distributable net income for such year, less amounts paid, credited or required to be distributed in such year.

The trustee makes this election by so indicating on the Form 1041 for each year when desired.

The effect of this rule on the beneficiary is that these delayed payments must be treated by him as having been received within the preceding taxable year, and they are taxable to him in that year.

THE TAX AND CREDITS

Upon completion of all the steps described up to this point, the tax return and all supporting schedules will have been filled in, down to the trust's taxable income (except that the Schedules K-1 will be only partially complete; there is more on this in the following section).

The amount of the tax can now be computed, using the tax rate schedule given on page 101.

Next, reference should be made to Chapter 6 for a checklist of possible additions to or credits against the tax. The Form 1041 also lists all of these very clearly.

The return should be signed by the trustee or his agent, and by the return preparer, and filed before the fifteenth day of the fourth month following the close of the trust's taxable year. It is filed with the Internal Revenue Service Center for the state where the trustee has his residence or principal place of business. The tax is due in full at the time of filing.

ALLOCATION OF DISTRIBUTIONS

It is sometimes necessary to make an allocation of the trust's distributions between two or more beneficiaries to determine the proper amount which will be taxable to each and to be able to show this amount on the Schedule K-1 given to each.

The maximum deduction for distributions is, again, limited to Distributable Net Income. If there is enough DNI to cover the distributions to all beneficiaries no allocation is necessary, but it often happens that the actual distributions during a year will exceed DNI. The question to be answered in this case is, to which beneficiaries shall the deductible portion of the distributions be taxed?

First, it should be remembered that all required distributions of current income plus *discretionary* distributions of current income plus payments from the trust *corpus* are deductible by the trust—and taxable to the beneficiaries—if they do not exceed DNI. But if they do exceed DNI, Code Section 662 allocates the DNI as follows:

1. Beneficiaries to whom specified portions of the current income are paid, credited, or required to be distributed are taxable on those portions—unless the combined portions of all the beneficiaries exceed the DNI for the taxable year (before any charitable contribution deduction).

If the combined portions do exceed the DNI, the taxable portion of each beneficiary shall equal:

$$\text{DNI} \times \frac{\text{Current income required to be distributed to him}}{\text{Current income required to be distributed to all beneficiaries.}}$$

2. Beneficiaries of discretionary current income or corpus payments will be taxable on amounts paid, credited, or required to be distributed to them to the extent these payments are attributable to Distributable Net Income.

To compute the taxable amount, the *required* current income distributions are first subtracted from Distributable Net Income; then, each beneficiary's taxable portion will equal:

$$\text{Remainder of DNI} \times \frac{\text{amount paid, credited, or required to be distributed to him}}{\text{amount paid, credited, or required to be distributed to all beneficiaries.}}$$

TIER DISTRIBUTIONS

The method of allocation summarized above is known as the "tier system." It classifies all amounts paid or payable to the beneficiaries into two tiers. The first tier includes currently distributable income and other amounts required to be paid from income or corpus to the extent they are actually paid from currently distributable income. The second tier includes all other amounts paid or payable to the beneficiary.

Two examples will illustrate and help to clarify the use of the tier system.*

> EXAMPLE 1. A trust is required to distribute one-half of its current income for the tax year to A, the grantor's son, one-quarter to B, the grantor's daughter, and one-quarter to C, a charity. The trust income is $10,000. The charitable contribution is $2,500, the amount required to be distributed to A is $5,000 and the amount required to be distributed to B is $2,500. Hence, the amount required to be distributed to all beneficiaries is $7,500, since the charity is not considered a beneficiary. Assume the distributable net income of the trust is $7,000 before the charitable deduction is taken. A will include $4,666.67 ($5,000/$7,500 x $7,000) in his gross income. B will include $2,333.33 ($2,500/$7,500 x $7,000) in her gross income.
>
> If the sum of the first and second tier distributions exceeds

---

*Federal Tax Guide, 1976, published by Prentice-Hall, Inc.

the distributable net income, the beneficiary must include in his gross income only a proportionate share of the distributable net income (less first tier distributions). His share is determined as follows:

$$\text{Distributable net income less first tier distributions} \times \frac{\text{second tier distributions to the beneficiary}}{\text{second tier distributions to all beneficiaries}} = \text{The beneficiary's share of distributable net income}$$

Thus, beneficiaries are taxed on second tier distributions only if the first tier distributions fail to exhaust the distributable net income of the trust. This is so, even if the distributions are made from income.

EXAMPLE 2. A trust requires the distribution annually of $8,000 of income to A. Any remaining income may be accumulated or distributed to B, C, and D in the trustee's discretion. He may also invade corpus for the benefit of A,B,C, or D. During the year, the trust has $20,000 income after deducting expenses. Distributable net income is $20,000. The trustee distributed $8,000 of income to A. He also distributes $4,000 each to B and C, $2,000 to D, and an additional $6,000 to A. The amount taxable to A, B, C, and D is determined as follows:

Distributable net income	$20,000
Less: first tier distribution to A	8,000
Available for second tier distributions	$12,000
Second tier distributions:	
A — 6,000/16,000 x $12,000	$ 4,500
B — 4,000/16,000 x $12,000	3,000
C — 4,000/16,000 x $12,000	3,000
D — 2,000/16,000 x $12,000	1,500

A includes $12,500 in income ($8,000 first tier distribution plus $4,500 second tier distribution). B and C each include $3,000 in income, and D includes $1,500.

THE SEPARATE SHARE RULE

In determining the amount taxable to the beneficiaries, allocation by tiers may work an injustice when a trust is administered in substantially separate shares.

Suppose, for example, that a trust with two beneficiaries has distributable net income of $20,000. The trustee makes a mandatory distribution of one-half this amount, or $10,000 to beneficiary A. He accumulates the other $10,000 for future distribution to B. He also makes a discretionary distribution of $10,000 out of corpus to A as an annuitant. Under the tier system the entire distributable net income would be allocated to A, and A would be taxed on the $20,000 received. His tax is being measured, in part, by $10,000 of income that can only go to B.

Suppose now that we divide the above trust into two separate trusts, one for each beneficiary. Each trust will have distributable net income of $10,000. The trustee of the trust for A distributes all the income of the trust and $10,000 of the corpus to A. The trustee of the trust for B makes no distributions. Under these facts, A would be taxed on $10,000. He actually received $20,000, but his taxable share may not exceed the distributable net income of his trust. The B trust made no distributions, and so its income of $10,000 is taxable to the trustee.*

The separate share device is a device for achieving the two-trust result in a one-trust case. Section 663 (c) states in effect that for the sole purpose of determining the deductions allowable to trusts and the gross income of their beneficiaries in the case of a single trust having more than one beneficiary, "substantially separate and independent shares of different beneficiaries in the trust shall be treated as separate trusts."

The purpose of the separate share treatment, which is mandatory, is to prevent a beneficiary from being taxed on income accumulated for the other beneficiary of the trust.

DISTRIBUTION SCHEDULE FOR BENEFICIARIES

After making an allocation of the amounts distributed, if necessary, the Schedule K-1, "Beneficiary's Share of Income, Deductions, Credits, etc." may be completed.

On account of the conduit principle—income distributed retains the same character in the hands of a beneficiary that it had in the trust—each different kind of income must be reported by the beneficiary as the kind of income it was originally. That is, dividends, short-term capital gains, long-term capital gains, and others will be shown as such on the beneficiary's tax return. Also, certain deductions, such as depreciation, are reportable by the beneficiary.

Therefore, the Schedule K-1 must show each kind of income separately

---

* **Federal Tax Guide,** 1976, published by Prentice-Hall, Inc.

so that the beneficiary may report it properly. When this form is complete, the trust tax return is complete.

TAXATION OF THE BENEFICIARIES

Any difficulties in determining the amounts and kinds of income taxable to the beneficiaries must be resolved by the trustee, leaving the beneficiaries with little or no problem in showing their taxable shares of the distributions on their individual tax returns.

Each beneficiary will report his share of the total dividends along with any other dividends he might have on his Schedule B, showing that they came from the named trust, and his total dividends will be subject to the full $100 exclusion, regardless of how much dividend exclusion might have been used by the trust; capital gains are shown as either short-term or long-term on his Schedule D, and if they, along with his other capital gains and losses net out to a long-term capital gain he will use the fifty percent capital gain deduction; ordinary income from the trust will be shown on his Schedule E, with any depreciation allowable to him being deducted in the same place; and any other type of income will find its way to the proper place for that type of income on the individual return.

Upon termination of the trust, there are likely to be several other, more unusual, items the beneficiary will have to report; these are discussed in the following chapter, on terminations.

THE BENEFICIARY'S TAXABLE YEAR

A beneficiary must report his income from the trust for the trust's taxable year ending with or within his taxable year. The rule is the same as for a partner and his partnership.

In the case of a beneficiary who dies or terminates during the year there is a special rule in Regulations Section 1.652(c)-2, -3, -4 for determining the proper amount to report on the final return.

9

TERMINATION OF
TRUSTS

The termination of a trust brings up several questions and problems not encountered during the years of its life.

It is important to determine the exact cut-off date of the termination, both for fiduciary accounting and reporting purposes and for tax purposes; the two may not always be the same.

Also, the impact on the beneficiaries can be different in the year of termination from that in earlier years.

TIMING THE TERMINATION

There is not always any clear-cut advantage in having the trust terminate at one time rather than another, but in a few cases the time should be considered, so a summary of the rules might be helpful at this point.

A trust usually terminates at whatever time was specified in the trust instrument. Sometimes a certain date is given for termination, but it might depend on the happening of a certain event, such as the death of some person.

The law recognizes that the termination and settlement cannot take place instantaneously and allows a reasonable time for winding up the trust's affairs before demanding a final reporting.

For tax purposes, the regulations are a little more explicit, and they say that whether a trust has terminated depends on whether the property held in trust has been distributed to the persons entitled to succeed to it rather than on the technicality of whether or not the trustee has rendered his final accounting. A trust does not automatically terminate upon the happening of the event by which the duration of the trust is measured. A reasonable time is permitted after such event for the trustee to perform the duties necessary to complete the administration of the trust. Thus, if under the terms of the governing instrument the trust is to terminate upon the death of the life beneficiary and the corpus is to be distributed to the remainderman, the trust continues after the death of the life beneficiary for a period reasonably necessary to a proper winding up of the affairs of the trust. However, the winding up of a trust cannot be unduly postponed, and if the distribution of the trust corpus is unreasonably delayed, the trust is considered terminated for tax purposes after the expiration of a reasonable period for the trustee to complete the administration of the trust. Further, a trust will be considered as terminated when all the assets have been distributed except for a reasonable amount which is set aside in good faith for the payment of unascertained or contingent liabilities and expenses.

The purpose of this regulation is, of course, to prevent the trust from continuing longer than necessary just in order to keep alive a separate taxable entity, in case that might be advantageous tax-wise.

But since the trustee does have a little leeway in timing the termination, he should consider the tax consequences of different times for terminating the trust.

Assuming, for example, that the trust and its beneficiaries both report on a calendar year and that the trust is in a lower bracket than the beneficiaries, termination and distribution shortly before the end of the year would mean that the entire trust income would be taxable to the beneficiaries in that year; the year's entire income is generally considered to be included in the final distribution. If a portion of the income would ordinarily be taxable to the trust, timing the termination into the following year could save some taxes.

It is often necessary to liquidate some or all of the assets of an estate before terminating it, but this is not usually true with trusts. Most often, the trust's assets are simply distributed to the remaindermen in kind, and this creates no tax problem. Distribution of appreciated assets as part of the trust principal does not result in income to the trust or to the beneficiaries.

TIMING EXPENSES AND DISTRIBUTIONS

Every trust is different, so it is not possible to enumerate everything which a trustee might well consider in every situation, but a couple of examples of some possibilities might be helpful.

Suppose a terminating trust is in a lower bracket than the remainderman. Normally, the payment of expenses should be deferred, if possible, until the year of distribution since the deduction for them is relatively more valuable to a higher bracket taxpayer, either in the form of a reduction in the DNI of the trust in the year of the terminating distribution or as an excess deduction, or both.

Next, assume that a terminating trust contains $100,000 in common stock paying $5,000 a year in dividends and $100,000 in municipal bonds paying $5,000 a year in interest. Administration expenses for the year will be $5,000. The trustee believes that a final distribution will not be possible for at least a year, but that he can safely distribute half the corpus immediately. Should he distribute the stock or the bonds? He should distribute the bonds. Since the expenses of a trust must be allocated to taxable and tax-exempt income and are deductible only to the extent they are allocated to taxable income, it makes more sense to distribute the bonds and not lose the expense deduction. If the bonds are distributed the remainderman will have $5,000 of exempt income; the trust will have $5,000 of taxable income offset by $5,000 of expenses. If the stock was distributed instead, the trust would have nothing but tax-exempt income and the expense deduction would be lost entirely, and the remainderman would have taxable dividends on the stock without any benefit of the trust's expenses.

DISPOSITION OF CAPITAL LOSS CARRYOVERS

A trust's capital losses cannot be passed through to the beneficiaries at any time during the life of the trust. They may only be used as capital loss carryovers by the trust itself, subject to the usual rules for such carryovers.

But any unused capital loss carryovers remaining at the time of termination of the trust can be passed to the beneficiaries, who may then use them as capital loss carryovers on their individual returns.

The trust's current capital gains and losses, plus any capital loss carryover from prior years, will first be shown on its final return. If there is a net capital loss, it will be used to the extent of $1,000 (more after 1976) against the trust income for that year; any remaining loss will be allocated among the beneficiaries and will be reported to them (as either short-term or long-term losses, or both) on their Schedule K-1 (by showing them as losses on the lines for capital gains).

A beneficiary may use this loss on his Schedule D for his taxable year in which the trust ends. From then on, it will be treated just as if it were a capital loss he had incurred.

NET OPERATING LOSSES ON TERMINATION

A trust's net operating loss is another item which cannot be passed through to the beneficiaries except in the year of the trust's termination.

As explained earlier, a net operating loss must be used only by the trust, first as a carryback (if elected) then as a carryover, subject to the usual rules.

But on termination, if the five-year (or seven-year) carryover period has not expired, any remaining unused net operating loss carryover may be picked up by the beneficiaries. This, too, will be reported to the beneficiaries on their Schedules K-1, by showing the proper proportion for each beneficiary on a blank line of that schedule and identifying it as "N.O.L. Carryover."

A beneficiary may use this loss as a deduction *for* adjusted gross income, and he may continue to carry it forward, if necessary, for the remainder of the original term.

TAX YEARS AVAILABLE FOR LOSS CARRYOVER

The rules for determining the proper years to which a net operating loss may be carried are given in Regulations Section 1.642(h)-1, which say that the last taxable year of the trust and the same taxable year of the beneficiary must be considered as two different taxable years in making the determination.

This rule seems unreasonable, of course, and it was held to be unreasonable by the Second Circuit Court of Appeals (Dorfman v Comm., 394 F2d 651), but the regulation is still being followed by the Internal Revenue Service.

But if a trust's last year is the final year for a net operating loss carryover, any remaining unused carryover is not necessarily lost; the unused portion can be treated as an "excess deduction," described in the following section, by the beneficiary.

EXCESS DEDUCTIONS ON TERMINATION

When a trust has deductions—other than the personal exemption deduction and the charitable deduction—in excess of its income in any taxable year except its final year, this excess deduction is simply lost. It may not be carried back or forward, nor may it be passed through to the beneficiaries.

But excess deductions in the year of the trust's termination can be used by the beneficiaries who truly bear their burden, and the allocation of such deductions among several beneficiaries is prorated, based on the extent they share the financial burden, as required by Regulations Section 1.642(h)-4.

These excess deductions, including, possibly, any net operating loss carryover which cannot be used in the normal way, should be shown on the Schedule K-1 for each beneficiary; also, a schedule should be attached to the trust's tax return showing the computation of the deduction and the allocation to the beneficiaries.

USE OF EXCESS DEDUCTIONS BY BENEFICIARIES

Although a capital loss carryover and a net operating loss carryover may be used by a beneficiary, on termination, as deductions in arriving at adjusted gross income, the excess deductions allowable to a beneficiary may be used only in computing taxable income, not adjusted gross income; they are lost if the beneficiary does not itemize his deductions.

And these deductions may be used only in the beneficiary's taxable year in which the trust ends.

10

TAXATION OF ACCUMULATION DISTRIBUTIONS

As already noted, income distributed or distributable by a trust is taxed to the beneficiaries; undistributed income is taxed to the trust. Thus, it is not difficult to see that, without some special rules, distributions and accumulations of income could be manipulated to reduce the overall tax payable on a given amount of income by having the trust accumulate and pay the tax on the income rather than distribute it to a beneficiary in a higher tax bracket.

Then, when the income is distributed in a later year, along with the DNI for that year, little or no additional tax would otherwise be paid by the beneficiary, because distributions in excess of DNI are tax exempt to him.

But there is a tax rule, known as the ''throwback rule,'' the purpose of which is to prevent such shifts, and this rule applies only to complex trusts (though a simple trust that makes an accumulation distribution attributable to income of an earlier year is treated as a complex trust for that year).

The operation of the throwback rule—just because it exists and prevents taxpayers from trying to take the tax advantage they might otherwise try to obtain—is not a very common occurrence in the income taxation of trusts.

There have been several changes in the laws governing the taxation of accumulation distributions in recent years, so it should be emphasized that this chapter contains, first, the provisions which were in effect under the Tax Reform Act of 1969 and, next, a description of the relatively few changes brought about by the enactment of the Tax Reform Act of 1976.

THE THROWBACK RULE

Amounts distributed in any year in excess of current DNI—to the extent they constitute income accumulated but not previously distributed during preceding years—are called "accumulation distributions," and the throwback rule taxes the beneficiaries as if the amounts had been distributed each year instead of accumulated. There is no limit to the number of "preceding years" from which the distribution can be deemed to have been made, except that only taxable years beginning after December 31, 1968 may be considered.

The rule, which is covered in great detail in Code Sections 665-669 and the regulations thereunder, provides that the accumulation distribution *and* the amount of taxes paid by the trust with respect to the accumulated income are taxed to the beneficiary in the year he receives the distribution. His additional tax due to the distribution is computed in a way which will result in an approximation of the taxes he would have paid if he had received the distributions in the year or years the income was earned by the trust. (For distributions in the years beginning after December 31, 1968, the year when the trust earned the income is determined on a first-in, first-out basis.) The increase in tax as a result of this recomputation is a liability of the year the distribution is received. The total resulting increase in the beneficiary's tax generally will not exceed the total increase in tax he would have had to pay if the distribution had in fact occurred in the years the income was earned by the trust.

Also, the rule provides that the trust does not get a refund of taxes on the income later taxed to the beneficiary. The beneficiary, however, gets a tax credit for the amount of taxes the trust would have saved in prior years if it had in fact distributed the income in the year earned. Further, he can use any excess credit against taxes imposed on his income from other sources, and, under the 1969 law, if he then still had an excess, he could claim a refund.

THE ACCUMULATION DISTRIBUTION

For the throwback rule to come into play, there must first be an accumulation distribution in the current year.

An accumulation distribution generally occurs when a trust distributes an amount more than its DNI for the year. But, to define the term more precisely, an accumulation distribution means the amount by which any amounts properly paid, credited, or required to be distributed for a taxable year exceed the distributable net income for that year, reduced (but not below zero), by any amount of income for such taxable year required to be distributed currently (including any amount required to be distributed which may be paid out of income or corpus to the extent such amount is paid out of income for such taxable year).

UNDISTRIBUTED NET INCOME

Next, this excess distribution must be "thrown back" to the earliest year after 1968 that the trust had any undistributed net income, and so on through succeeding years up to the year of the accumulation distribution.

This means that an analysis of the distributions in prior years must be made to determine in which year or years there was any undistributed net income, defined as follows: the amount by which the DNI of the trust for the prior year exceeds the sum of the amount of income for such year required to be distributed currently, and any other amounts properly paid, credited, or required to be distributed for that year, and the amount of taxes imposed on the trust attributable to such distributable net income.

The accumulation distribution, then, will be considered as having been distributed in those years, chronologically, which had enough undistributed income to absorb it.

TAX ADDED TO DISTRIBUTIONS

When an accumulation distribution is thrown back to a particular year, all or part of the tax imposed on the trust for that year is also deemed distributed. This is done because the accumulation deemed distributed in the prior year would have increased the trust's distribution deduction in that year and thereby reduced or eliminated the trust's tax.

If the distribution thrown back is at least as much as the undistributed net income for that year, the tax paid by the trust for that year is eliminated and is, therefore, added to the distribution. If the distribution is less than that prior year's undistributed net income, the portion of the tax added to the accumulation distribution is determined as follows:

$$\text{Tax on the trust for the year to which the throwback is made} \quad \times \quad \frac{\text{Accumulation distribution thrown back to the particular year}}{\text{Undistributed net income for that particular year}} \quad = \quad \text{The amount of the tax deemed to have been distributed on the last day of that particular year}$$

TAX-EXEMPT INCOME THROWN BACK

If the undistributed part of the DNI for the year to which the distribution is thrown back includes any amount allocable to tax-exempt income, the income thrown back must be reduced by that amount in order not to tax the exempt part.

COMPLETION OF SCHEDULE

After making the above required determinations, the trustee will complete a Schedule J, Form 1041, Allocation of Accumulation Distribution.

To illustrate the use of this schedule, assume that a trust's 1975 distributions were $4,200 in excess of its 1975 DNI. An analysis of its prior years' distributions discloses that in only one previous year, the year 1973, was there any undistributed net income, which amounted to $6,101.24, and that the proportionate part of the trust's 1973 tax applicable to the 1975 accumulation distribution amounted to $949.12. Assume also that $468.10 of the distribution consisted of tax-exempt income.

The Schedule J will be completed as shown on page 145.

There must be a break-down of the various types of income deemed distributed, and if there is more than one beneficiary, each should be listed, with his proper portion of each item being shown.

CAPITAL GAIN DISTRIBUTIONS
(1969 LAW)

Under the 1969 law, if the current year's accumulation distribution was not absorbed by the undistributed *ordinary* income of all prior years, the excess was then thrown back against **undistributed** capital gains

SCHEDULE J (Form 1041) Department of the Treasury Internal Revenue Service	**Allocation of Accumulation Distribution** (For domestic complex trusts which in 1975 distributed income accumulated in earlier years) (Under sections 665 through 669 of the Internal Revenue Code)	19**75**

Name of trust	Employer identification number
XYZ Trust	62-0472080

1 Accumulation distribution in 1975 . . . . . ▶ $

To the extent of undistributed net income in preceding years, this amount must be thrown back to preceding years beginning with the earliest applicable year. If additional year columns are needed, attach additional copies of Schedule J (Form 1041).

	19.7.0	19.7.1	19.7.2	19.7.3.	19.7.4
Computation of amounts deemed distributed to beneficiaries					
2 Undistributed net income (adjust for prior throwbacks, if any)				6,101.24	
3 Throwback (line 1 but not more than line 2) . . .				4,200.00	
(NOTE: If this form shows a throwback to more than 1 year, enter only the balance of line 1 (line 1 minus line 3 of preceding column) in succeeding columns.)					
4 Taxes imposed on the trust applicable to amount on line 3 and deemed distributed				949.12	
5 Income and taxes deemed distributed (line 3 plus line 4)				5,149.12	
6 Tax-exempt income included in amount on line 5 .				468.10	
7 Taxable income deemed distributed (line 5 minus line 6)				4,681.02	

Enter the character of the amount on line 7 in columns 16 and 17 below for each beneficiary.

8 Capital gain distribution in 1975 . . . . . ▶ $

To the extent of undistributed capital gain in preceding years, this amount must be thrown back to preceding years beginning with the earliest applicable year. If additional year columns are needed, attach additional copies of Schedule J (Form 1041).

	19....	19....	19....	19....	19....
Computation of amounts deemed distributed to beneficiaries					
9 Undistributed capital gain					
10 Throwback (line 8 but not more than line 9) . . .					
11 Taxes imposed on the trust applicable to amount on line 10 and deemed distributed					
12 Capital gains and taxes deemed distributed (line 10 plus line 11)					

Enter the character of the amount on line 12 in columns 19 and 20 below for each beneficiary.

Allocation to beneficiaries

If more than one column above is used, either adjust the schedule below to indicate the character of distributions for each year, or attach a separate schedule showing such separate distribution. The beneficiary may use Form 4970 to compute the tax on the allocation and to claim credit for the share of the taxes deemed distributed by the trust.

	13. Name of each beneficiary	14. Social security number	15. Address
a	Frances Y. Johnson	338-10-7371	4126 New York Avenue,
b			Palm Beach, Fla., 33433
c			
d			

	16. Income from line 7 taxable to beneficiaries less the part reportable in column 17	17. Dividends (amount before exclusion)	18. Line 4 taxes deemed distributed	19. Net short-term capital gain	20. Net long-term capital gain (100%)	21. Line 11 taxes deemed distributed
a	2,808.62	1,872.40	949.12			
b						
c						
d						
Totals						

allocated to corpus, if any, for the preceding years starting after 1968. This means that there was a separate throwback for capital gains and that all other types of income for the preceding years starting after 1968 were deemed distributed before any amount of capital gain was deemed distributed.

If there was a capital gain throwback, the amount of taxes imposed on the trust in the throwback year which were attributable to such gains were also deemed distributed. When all of the undistributed capital gains of a preceding year were deemed distributed, all of the taxes imposed on the trust for such capital gains were also deemed distributed. When less than all of the undistributed capital gains were deemed distributed, the taxes deemed distributed would be the pro rata portion of the taxes imposed on the trust for such capital gains.

The capital gains distributions, as well as the tax on them, were shown separately for each beneficiary on the Schedule J so that he could report them properly on his individual tax return.

TAXATION OF THE BENEFICIARIES (1969 LAW)

Under the 1969 law, a beneficiary could elect either of two methods—the exact method or the shortcut method—for computing his tax for the year in which an accumulation distribution was made.

THE EXACT METHOD

If the exact method was used, a complete, exact recomputation of the beneficiary's tax had to be made for each prior year affected by the throwback. Actual income figures used originally for each year were adjusted by the amount of the distribution deemed to have come from that year (plus the trust's taxes paid on it), and a tax was computed on the new taxable income. The difference between that new tax and the tax originally paid for that year was added to the regular tax for the current year (accumulation distribution year).

Form 4970, Tax on Accumulation Distribution of Trusts, shown on page 147, provided a convenient worksheet for making the necessary recomputations, and it was attached to the beneficiary's current tax return. (If more than five years were affected by the throwback, an additional Form 4970 could be used.)

Form **4970** (Rev. Oct. 1975) Department of the Treasury Internal Revenue Service	**Tax on Accumulation Distribution of Trusts** For calendar year 19........., or other taxable year beginning ...., 19........ and ending ...., 19........	Attach to Beneficiary's Tax Return

Name(s) as shown on return	Social security number

Name and address of trust	Identifying number

Type of trust ☐ Domestic ☐ Foreign	Method used in computing the tax adjustment ☐ Exact ☐ Shortcut (see instruction 4(b))	Taxable distribution ☐ Net income ☐ Capital gain

PART I.—Average Income for Shortcut Method (Exclude Tax Exempt Income)

1 Number of trust's preceding taxable years in which amount distributed was accumulated . . . .
2 (a) Total undistributed amount deemed distributed for the years on line 1 . . . . . .
  (b) Less: Dividend exclusion or 50% capital gain deduction applicable to amounts on line 2(a) . . . . .
3 Total taxes imposed on the trust attributable to amount on line 2(a). (See instruction 2(c).) . . . . . .
4 Combine amounts on lines 2 and 3 . . . .
5 Average of taxable portion deemed distributed (divide line 4 by line 1) . . . .
6 Enter 25% of line 5 . . . .
7 Number of years on line 1 in which amount deemed distributed is not less than the amount on line 6 . . . .
8 Average amount for recomputing tax (divide line 4 by line 7). Enter on line 12 in columns for 1st, 2d, and 3d years

PART II.—Computation of Tax Attributable to the Accumulation Distribution (Exclude Tax Exempt Income)

Note: *If you use the Shortcut Method disregard lines 10 and 11 and columns for the 4th and 5th prior years.*

	Beneficiary's Prior Taxable Years				
	5th year	4th year	3d year	2d year	1st year
9 Adjusted gross income or (loss). (See instruction 5(b).)					
10 Enter undistributed amount deemed distributed less any dividend exclusion or 50% capital gain deduction applicable to amount distributed					
11 Taxes imposed on the trust on amount distributed .					
12 Average amount for shortcut method (from line 8) .	///////	///////			
13 Combine lines 9, 10, and 11 or lines 9 and 12 . .					
14 Standard deduction, or itemized deductions . . .					
15 Exemption deduction allowable					
16 Total deductions (add lines 14 and 15)					
17 Taxable income as corrected (line 13 less 16) . .					
18 Tax as corrected. (See instruction 5(e).)					
19 Tax surcharge (where applicable)					
20 Total tax (add lines 18 and 19)					
21 Tax credits allowable. (See instruction 5(f).) . .					
22 Tax after credits (line 20 less 21)					
23 Tax, less nonrefundable tax credits, on line 9 income					
24 Tax attributable to distribution (line 22 less 23) .					
25 Minimum tax adjustment. (See instruction 5(h).) .					
26 Total tax (combine lines 24 and 25)					
27 Taxes paid by trust (from line 11)					
28 Net tax adjustment (line 26 less 27)					

29 Net tax adjustment for exact method attributable to distribution (combine amounts on line 28 and enter in Part III) . . . . .

SHORTCUT METHOD—Use Lines 30 through 33.

30 Average tax attributable to distribution (combine amounts for 1st, 2d and 3d prior years on line 26 and divide by 3) . . .
31 Multiply tax on line 30 by number of years on line 7 . . . .
32 Taxes imposed on the trust attributable to amount distributed (from line 3) . . . .
33 Net tax adjustment (subtract line 32 from 31 and enter in Part III) . . . .

PART III.—Computation of Net Tax Adjustment

34 Partial tax or (overpayment) attributable to ordinary income (from line 29 or 33) . . . .
35 Partial tax or (overpayment) attributable to capital gains (from line 29 or 33). (See instruction 1.) . . . .
36 Net tax adjustment (combine lines 34 and 35). Individuals enter amount on Form 1040, page 1, as instructed in (a) and (b) below:
  (a) **Partial tax**—Include in Tax (line before any tax credits) and write to the right of the entry space "Accumulation Distribution Tax."
  (b) **Overpayment of tax**—Include in Total for payments and write to the left of the entry space "Throwback credit."
  (Beneficiaries other than individuals enter amount on the comparable line of the Income Tax return they file.)

Form **4970** (Rev. 10–75)

THE SHORTCUT METHOD

The shortcut method averaged the tax attributable to the thrown-back distribution over the years in which the trust earned the income. A fraction of the distribution based on the number of years in which the income was accumulated was included in the beneficiary's income in each of the three years immediately preceding the year of distribution. The additional tax for each of the three years was actually computed and an average yearly additional tax determined. This amount was multiplied by the number of years to which the income distributed related, and the result was the additional tax liability due and payable for the year in which the accumulation distribution took place (subject to the credit for taxes paid by the trust).

The Form 4970 was used, also, if the shortcut method was elected.

Obviously, the shortcut method was a little easier to use than the exact method, and it was the only method possible if the beneficiary's tax returns for years prior to the three preceding years were not available.

To illustrate the use of the shortcut method under the 1969 law, assume that a trust had accumulated income of $12,000 over a period of twelve years and had paid taxes totalling $2,000 on the accumulation; the entire income of $10,000 net was paid to a beneficiary in the year 1975.

The beneficiary is deemed to have received not only the $10,000 but the $2,000 as well, for a total of $12,000. The $12,000 is taxed as follows:

1. Divide the accumulation distribution of $12,000 by 12, the number of years in which the income was accumulated, $1,000.

2. Recompute the beneficiary's tax for each of his three preceding years after adding $1,000 to his income for each year. Assume that his taxes would have been increased by,

First preceding year	$300.00
Second preceding year	400.00
Third preceding year	200.00
Total	$900.00

3. Divide this total by three to find the average yearly tax increase, $300.

4. Multiply the average yearly tax increase, $300, by the number of years in the accumulation period, 12, for a total of $3,600, the additional tax due on the accumulation distribution, which will be reduced by the $2,000 tax paid by the trust itself.

The exact method and the shortcut method were also used to compute the tax on capital gains distributions. A beneficiary receiving an accumulation distribution of both ordinary income and capital gains did not have to use the same method in computing his tax as to each. He could compute his tax on the ordinary income distribution under the exact method and his tax on the capital gain distribution under the shortcut method, or vice versa.

The shortcut method could not be used by a beneficiary if during any of his preceding taxable years to which the current distribution was thrown back, prior accumulation distributions also were thrown back by two or more *other* trusts. This provision was intended to prevent the creation of multiple trusts with staggered accumulation distributions to take advantage of the shortcut rule.

And, finally, if a beneficiary was not in existence during a year in which income was accumulated, either computation method could be used, and it was assumed that he had no other income, was on the calendar year basis, was single, and had one personal exemption.

The total additional tax due, as computed under either method, had to be added to the beneficiary's regular tax for the distribution year, with the notation, "Accumulation Distribution Tax." The tax credit to which he was entitled would be shown on Line 22 of his Form 1040 (1975) with "Throwback Credit" written to the left of the entry.

TAX REFORM ACT OF 1976

Under the Tax Reform Act of 1976 the throwback rules remain the same in general as under the 1969 law—the definition of an accumulation distribution is the same, the tax paid by the trust is still added to the distribution, tax-exempt income is treated the same as before, and so on. But the Act did make several important changes in the taxation of accumulation distributions.

<u>Taxation of Beneficiaries</u>—The most important of these changes had to do with the method of computing a beneficiary's tax on a distribution.

The use of two alternative methods (exact and shortcut) proved so complex that a single simplified method, similar to the old shortcut method, is now provided for, and it applies to distributions made in taxable years beginning after December 31, 1975. The computation is made as follows:

1. Divide the accumulation distribution (plus the tax paid by the trust) by the number of years in which the income was accumulated by the trust (as under the 1969 law).
2. Of the beneficiary's five taxable years immediately preceding the distribution year, eliminate the year with the lowest taxable income and the year with the highest taxable income.
3. To each of the three remaining taxable years add the percentage of the distribution determined in (1) above.
4. Recompute the beneficiary's tax for each of these three years based on the new taxable income figure and determine the tax increase for each year.
5. Add the three tax increases together and divide by three to obtain the average yearly additional tax.
6. Multiply this average yearly additional tax by the number of years in which the income was accumulated by the trust, the same number as in (1) above.

The result is the beneficiary's tax on the accumulation distribution which must be included on his tax return for the year in which he receives the distribution. As before, however, he may then claim a credit for the taxes paid by the trust, but if the tax credit exceeds the liability there is no longer any refund made.

Accumulations for Minors—The 1976 law also provides that, for distributions made after 1975, accumulations for people before they are born and for children up to age 21 are exempt from the throwback rules taxing accumulations to the beneficiaries upon receipt. But this benefit extends only to the first two trusts if the child is a beneficiary of three or more trusts.

Capital Gain Accumulations—Finally, the 1976 law makes an important change affecting capital gain accumulations. There is no longer any throwback tax on capital gains. They may be ignored completely. There is, however, a new special rule in connection with capital gains which covers possible abuse where a grantor places in trust property which has unrealized appreciation, as explained in Chapter 8.

11

A COMPLETE
TRUST ACCOUNTING
CASE STUDY ILLUSTRATED

To better illustrate many of the principles of trust accounting, reporting, and taxation discussed earlier, this chapter presents a study of a complete case.

A fairly typical complex trust is followed from its creation through its accounting procedures and to the detailed completion of its tax return at the end of its first year.

FACTS OF THE CASE*

An irrevocable inter-vivos trust was created by Robert Madison on January 1, 1976. He placed half of his property in this trust, his objectives being to save income taxes over the years by diverting a portion of his in-

---

*Adapted, with permission, from **Income Taxation of Estates and Trusts**, American Institute of CPA's, New York, New York, 1976.

come to lower-bracket taxpayers, to help his favorite charity for many years, possibly even after his death, and to provide income for his two children while withholding any large amount of property from them until they would be more likely to know how to handle it wisely.

Mr. Madison named Harry Douglas as trustee (with the National Bank and Trust Company as successor trustee) and transferred the following property to the trust:

Cash	$100,000.00
Corporate Bonds	250,000.00
Municipal Bonds	80,000.00
Office Building	150,000.00
Total	$580,000.00

The trust was established to exist for a period of twenty years. At the end of that time, one-half of the trust principal is to be distributed to Mr. Madison's son, James Madison, now 24, and the other half to his daughter, Eleanor Madison, now 20.

The trust instrument provides that, each year, ten percent of the trust income shall be distributed to the Salvation Army and that one-half of the remainder of the trust income shall be distributed to the son, James Madison. The trustee is given discretionary power to either accumulate the balance of the income or to distribute additional amounts to James Madison and to distribute any portion of the remainder that he sees fit to the daughter, Eleanor Madison.

The trust instrument further provides that there is to be no provision for depreciation and that all capital gains and losses shall be attributable to corpus rather than to income; also that eighty percent of the administrative expenses shall be charged to income and twenty percent to principal.

THE ACCOUNTING SYSTEM

After qualifying as trustee and receiving the trust property, Harry Douglas set up a simple set of books for the trust. A general ledger was opened with the following accounts, including those needed at present and those expected to be needed in the future:

Assets:

   101—Principal Cash
   102—Income Cash
   103—Corporate Bonds
   104—Municipal Bonds
   105—Corporate Stock
   106—Office Building

Net Worth (Principal):

   300—Trust Principal

   400—Gains Applicable to Principal
   401—Losses Applicable to Principal
   402—Administrative Expenses—Principal
   404—Distributions of Principal

Net Worth (Income):

   500—Trust Income
   600—Distributions of Income

Income:

   700—Tax-Exempt Interest
   701—Taxable Interest
   703—Rental Income
   704—Other Income

Expenses:

   800—Administrative Expenses
   801—Rental Expenses
   802—Income Taxes Paid

A combination journal was started, with the following columnar headings:

   Date
   Payee or Explanation
   Check Number or Receipt Number
   Principal Cash—Debit
   Principal Cash—Credit
   Income Cash—Debit
   Income Cash—Credit
   Tax-Exempt Interest—Credit
   Taxable Interest—Credit
   Rental Income—Credit
   Other Income—Credit
   Administrative Expenses—Debit
   Rental Expenses—Debit
   Other Accounts—Acct. No.
       —Debit
       —Credit

The ledger, the combination journal, and a general journal constituted the accounting system for this trust.

THE OPENING ENTRY

The opening entry for the set of books was made as follows:

Principal Cash	100,000.00	
Corporate Bonds	250,000.00	
Municipal Bonds	80,000.00	
Office Building	150,000.00	
Trust Principal	$580,000.00	

Each of the assets was recorded at its fair market value as of January, 1, 1976—the same values used by Mr. Madison on the gift tax return covering this transfer to the trust.

TRANSACTIONS FOR THE YEAR

Each transaction for the year 1976 was recorded in the combination journal; these are described as follows, and the entry for each is shown in general journal form:

1. One thousand shares of White Industries, Inc., common stock was purchased on January 20, 1976 for $85,000.00.

Corporate Stock	85,000.00	
Principal Cash		85,000.00

2. The above stock was sold on September 16, 1976 for $90,000.00.

Principal Cash	90,000.00	
Corporate Stock		85,000.00
Gains Applicable to Principal		5,000.00

3. Interest received on the corporate bonds during the year totalled $24,000.00.

Income Cash	24,000.00	
Taxable Interest		24,000.00

4. Interest received during the year on the municipal bonds was $4,000.00.

Income Cash	4,000.00	
Tax-Exempt Interest		4,000.00

5. Rents received from the office building during the year amounted to $15,000.00.

Income Cash	15,000.00	
Rental Income		15,000.00

6. The various expenses in connection with the rental property were $3,000.00 for the year.

Rental Expenses	3,000.00	
Income Cash		3,000.00

7. Total administrative expenses for the year were $1,000.00, allocated according to the directions in the trust instrument.

Administrative Expense—principal	200.00	
Administrative Expense	800.00	
Principal Cash		200.00
Income Cash		800.00

8. The trust's net income for the year was determined to be $39,200.00, so on December 31, 1976 the trustee made the required distributions of $3,920.00 (ten percent) to the Salvation Army and $17,640.00 (one-half of the balance) to James Madison.

Distribution of Income	21,560.00	
Income Cash		21,560.00

9. The trustee also made discretionary distributions to James Madison of $2,000.00 and to Eleanor Madison of $6,000.00.

Distributions of Income	8,000.00	
Income Cash		8,000.00

A trial balance of the trust's ledger at the end of the year is as follows:

	Debit	Credit
Principal Cash	104,800.00	
Income Cash	9,640.00	
Corporate Bonds	250,000.00	
Municipal Bonds	80,000.00	
Office Building	150,000.00	
Trust Principal		580,000.00
Gains Applicable to Principal		5,000.00
Administrative Expenses—Principal	200.00	
Trust Income		—
Distributions of Income	29,560.00	
Tax-Exempt Interest		4,000.00
Taxable Interest		24,000.00
Rental Income		15,000.00
Administrative Expenses	800.00	
Rental Expenses	3,000.00	
	628,000.00	628,000.00

THE CLOSING ENTRY

No adjusting entries are necessary at the end of the year (not even one for depreciation since, in this case, depreciation is not to be provided for), so the only entry needed is one to close the income and expense accounts into Trust Income.

Tax-Exempt Interest	4,000.00	
Taxable Interest	24,000.00	
Rental Income	15,000.00	
Administrative Expense		800.00
Rental Expenses		3,000.00
Trust Income		39,200.00

All other accounts, such as Gains Applicable to Principal and Distributions of Income, remain open and are closed only on the final termination of the trust.

INTERIM REPORT TO THE COURT

If year-end statements are needed, they can either be the usual Balance Sheet and Income Statement, the preparation of which would be a

ROBERT MADISON TRUST

Harry Douglas, Trustee

CHARGE AND DISCHARGE STATEMENT

For the Year Ended December 31, 1976

First as to Principal:

The Trustee Charges Himself With:

Assets Placed in Trust (Schedule A)	$580,000.00
Gains Applicable to Principal	5,000.00
	$585,000.00

The Trustee Credits Himself With:

Administrative Expenses Applicable to Principal	200.00
Leaving a Balance of Principal of	$584,800.00

Consisting of:

Cash in Bank	$104,800.00
Corporate Bonds	250,000.00
Municipal Bonds	80,000.00
Office Building	150,000.00
Total	$584,800.00

Second as to Income:

The Trustee Charges Himself With:

Tax-Exempt Interest Income	$ 4,000.00	
Taxable Interest Income	24,000.00	
Rental Income	15,000.00	$ 43,000.00

The Trustee Credits Himself With:

Administrative Expenses	$ 800.00	
Rental Expenses	3,000.00	
Distributions to Beneficiaries	29,560.00	33,360.00
Leaving a Balance of Income of		$ 9,640.00

Consisting of:

Cash in Bank	$ 9,640.00

Schedule A—Assets Placed in Trust:

Cash	$100,000.00
Corporate Bonds	250,000.00
Municipal Bonds	80,000.00
Office Building	150,000.00
Total	$580,000.00

very simple matter, or they can consist of a Charge and Discharge State-ment.

The Charge and Discharge Statement, described in Chapter 4, is considered better for a trust, and such a statement can also serve as an interim (or final) report to the court.

A Charge and Discharge Statement for the Robert Madison Trust at December 31, 1976 is shown on page 157.

TAX RETURN WORKSHEET

The trustee next proceeded to prepare the 1976 tax return for the trust. The fiduciary accounting income, which is his staring point, was determined above to be $39,200, and all other figures needed are readily available except one—the amount of allowable depreciation for the year, determined to be $2,000.

The first step, as usual, was to make any necessary allocations, and the first of these was the allocation of expenses to taxable and to tax-exempt income.

The $3,000 of rental expenses do not enter into the allocation, as they are directly attributable to the rental income and are fully deductible. But the $1,000 of administrative expenses, indirect expenses, are allocated on the basis of gross taxable income to gross fiduciary accounting income. Taxable income is the taxable interest of $24,000 plus gross rents of $15,000, or $39,000; total gross income consists of those two amounts plus $4,000 of tax-exempt interest, or $43,000. So, $1,000 multiplied by 39 and divided by 43 equals $907, the portion applicable to taxable income. The remainder, $93, is not deductible. (The $5,000 capital gain is not considered here, because the allocation of any indirect expense to an item excluded from the computation of distributable net income, such as capital gains credited to corpus, is precluded by Regulations Section 1.652(b)-3(b).)

Next, the amount of the charitable distribution attributable to the tax-exempt income must be determined. The same proportion is used as in the preceding paragraph, so, $3,920 multiplied by 39 and divided by 43 equals $3,555, the portion of the charitable contribution attributable to taxable in-

ROBERT MADISON TRUST
WORKSHEET FOR 1976 TRUST TAX RETURN

ALLOCATIONS REQUIRED

Expenses Attributable to Taxable Income 907.00
Expenses Attributable to Exempt Income 93.00

Charitable Deduction Attributable to Taxable Income 3,555.00
Charitable Deduction Attributable to Exempt Income 365.00

Depreciation Apportioned on Basis of Fiduciary
Accounting Income Allocated to Each:
 Salvation Army 200.00
 James Madison 1,002.00
 Eleanor Madison 306.00
 Trustee 492.00

FIDUCIARY ACCOUNTING INCOME

— Administrative Expenses Allocated to Corpus .... (200.00)
+ Capital Gains Belonging to Corpus 5,00.00
— Capital Gain Deduction of 50% .... (2,500.00)
— Tax-Exempt Income, Net of Allocated Expenses .... (3,907.00)
— Charitable Contributions Made from Income .... (3,920.00)
+ Portion of Contributions Attributable to Exempt INcome 365.00
— Depreciation Allocated to the Trust .... (492.00)
— The Personal Exemption .... (100.00)

= TAXABLE INCOME BEFORE DISTRIBUTIONS DEDUCTION 33,446.00

+ The Personal Exemption 100.00
+ Capital Gain Deduction of 50% 2,500.00
— Capital Gains Belonging to Corpus .... (5,000.00)
+ Tax-Exempt INcome, Net of Allocated Expenses 3,907.00
— Undeductible Portion of Contributions Due to Exempt Income .... (365.00)

= DISTRIBUTABLE NET INCOME 34,588.00

— Tax-Exempt Income, Net of Allocated Expenses and Portion
 of Contributions Attributable to Exempt Income .... (3,542.00)

= DISTRIBUTIONS DEDUCTION (Maximum, but see below) 31,046.00

The distributions deduction, however, is limited to actual distributions, 17,640 + 2,000 + 6,000 = 25,640, less exempt income
allocated thereto, 2,012 + 613 = 2,625, for a net distributions
deduction of $23,015.00.

TAXABLE INCOME BEFORE DISTRIBUTIONS DEDUCTION 33,446.00
 — Distributions Deduction .... (23,015.00)
= TAXABLE INCOME OF THE TRUST 10,431.00

come and therefore deductible. The remainder of the distribution, $365, is not deductible.

Finally, depreciation must be apportioned between each beneficiary and the trust itself on the basis of the share of net fiduciary accounting income allocated to each. The share of trust income allocated to the Salvation Army was $3,920, to James Madison $17,640 plus $2,000, or $19,640, to Eleanor Madison $6,000, and to the trust (undistributed) $9,640. So the $2,000 of depreciation is apportioned as follows:

Salvation Army	3,920/39,200 x $2,000 =	$ 200.00
James Madison	19,640/39,200 x $2,000 =	1,002.00
Eleanor Madison	6,000/39,200 x $2,000 =	306.00
Trustee	9,640/39,200 x $2,000 =	492.00
	39,200/39,200 x $2,000 =	$2,000.00

After these allocations are made, the tax worksheet may be completed, as shown on page 159.

In this case, since the actual distributions were less than the DNI reduced by tax-exempt income, the actual distribution will be the maximum amount deductible as a distributions deduction. But these actual distributions must further be reduced by the tax-exempt income included in them (Code Section 661(c)).

The computation of the tax-exempt income included in the distributions is shown in the following table, which also produces the figures needed in preparing the Schedule K-1 for each beneficiary.

	DNI	Per Cent	Taxable Interest	Net Rental Income	Net Tax Exempt Income
James Madison	$19,640.00	56.78%	$11,094.00	$ 6,534.00	$2,012.00
Eleanor Madison	6,000.00	17.35%	3,390.00	1,997.00	613.00
Trustee	8,948.00	25.87%	5,054.00	2,977.00	917.00
	$34,588.00	100.00%	$19,538.00	$11,508.00	$3,542.00
			(1)	(2)	(3)

(1) Taxable interest is the gross $24,000.00 less the administrative expenses applicable to it, $907.00, and less the charitable deduction applicable to it, $3,555.00, or $19,538.00.

(2)   The net rental income is the gross $15,000.00 less $3,000.00 of direct expenses and the trust's share of depreciation, $492.00, or $11,508.00.

(3)   The net tax-exempt income is the gross $4,000.00 less the $93.00 of administrative expenses allocated to it and less the $365.00 portion of the charitable deduction attributable to it, or $3,542.00.

The taxable income of the trust can be proved out by the following simple computation:

Trustee's Portion of DNI		$ 8,948.00
Capital Gain, Net of 50% Deduction		2,500.00
		$11,448.00
Less: Exemption	$100.00	
Tax-Exempt Interest Included in DNI	917.00	1,017.00
Taxable Income of the Trust		$10,431.00

THE TRUST'S TAX RETURN

After all of the required figures have been determined, as above, it is not difficult to transfer them to the tax return.

The 1976 tax return for the Robert Madison Trust will be completed as shown on the following pages.

There is included one form which has not been mentioned before, a Form 1041-A, which is an information return to be filed by any trust which claims a charitable deduction under Code Section 642(c). This return is not filed with the Form 1041 but is sent to the Internal Revenue Service Center, 11601 Roosevelt Boulevard, Philadelphia, Pennsylvania 19155.

U.S. Fiduciary Income Tax Return

Form **1041**

Department of the Treasury
Internal Revenue Service

for the year January 1–December 31, 1976, or other taxable year

beginning .... , 1976, and ending .... , 19......

1976

Check whether:
- ☐ Estate
- ☐ Simple trust
- ☒ Complex trust

If trust, check whether:
- ☐ Testamentary
- ☒ Inter vivos
- ☐ "Grantor type"

Also check if:
- ☐ Pooled income fund

Name of estate or trust ("Grantor type" trusts, see instruction O.)
Robert Madison Trust

Name and title of fiduciary
Harry Douglas, Trustee

Address of fiduciary (number and street)
206 Madison Building

City, State, and ZIP code
Anderson, Illinois 60642

Employer identification number
65-0427191

Nonexempt charitable and split-interest trusts check applicable boxes (See Inst. U.):
- ☐ Described in section 4947(a)(1)
- ☐ Not treated as a private foundation by reason of sec. 509(a) (1), (2) or (3)
- ☐ Described in section 4947(a)(2)

Is this the first return? ☐ Yes ☒ No. If "No," has the fiduciary's address changed? ☐ Yes ☐ No.

INCOME

1 Dividends (Enter full amount before exclusion)	1	
2 Interest	2	24,000.00
3 Income from partnerships and other fiduciaries	3	
4 Gross rents and royalties	4	15,000.00
5 Gross profit (loss) from trade or business	5	
6 Net gain (loss) from capital assets (Attach Schedule D (Form 1041))	6	5,000.00
7 Ordinary gains and (losses) (Attach Form 4797)	7	
8 Other income (State nature of income)	8	
9 Total income (lines 1 to 8, inclusive)	9	44,000.00

DEDUCTIONS

10 Interest	10	
11 Taxes	11	
12 Fiduciary's portion of depreciation (Schedule A) and depletion. Explain depletion	12	492.00
13 Charitable deduction (Schedule B, line 9)	13	3,555.00
14 Other deductions (Itemize) Rental Expenses 3,000.00 Administrative Expenses 907.00	14	3,907.00
15 Total (lines 10 to 14, inclusive)	15	7,954.00
16 Line 9 minus line 15 (Complex trusts and estates enter this amount in Schedule C, line 1 also)	16	36,046.00
17 Deduction for distributions to beneficiaries	17	23,015.00
18 Adjustment of dividend exclusion	18	
19 Federal estate tax attributable to income in respect of a decedent (Fiduciary's share)	19	
20 Long-term capital gain deduction. Enter 50% of Schedule D (Form 1041) line 17e	20	2,500.00
21 Exemption (If final return, see General Instruction M.)	21	100.00
22 Total (lines 17 to 21, inclusive)	22	25,615.00
23 Taxable income of fiduciary (line 16 minus line 22)	23	10,431.00

COMPUTATION OF TAX

24 Tax on amount on line 23 (See tax rate schedule)	24	2,327.92
25 If alternative tax is applicable, enter the tax from Schedule D (Form 1041) line 29	25	
26 Fiduciary's share of foreign tax credit (Attach Form 1116)	26	
27 Fiduciary's share of investment credit (Attach Form 3468)	27	
28 Fiduciary's share of work incentive (WIN) program credit (Attach Form 4874)	28	
29 Total (lines 26 to 28, inclusive)	29	
30 Balance (line 24 or 25, whichever is applicable, less line 29)	30	2,327.92
31 Tax from recomputing fiduciary's share of prior year investment credit (Attach Form 4255)	31	
32 Minimum tax (Attach Form 4626)	32	
33 Total (lines 30 to 32, inclusive)	33	
34 Fiduciary's share of credit for tax paid at source on tax-free convenant bond interest	34	
35 Credit for Federal tax on special fuels, nonhighway gas and lub. oil (Attach Form 4136)	35	
36 Credit from regulated investment companies (Attach Form 2439)	36	
37 Tax previously paid (See Instruction 37 and attach Form 2758)	37	
38 Federal income tax withheld (Attach Form W–2)	38	
39 Total (lines 34 to 38, inclusive)	39	
40 Balance of tax due (line 33 less line 39)	40	2,327.92
41 Overpayment (line 39 less line 33)	41	

Under penalties of perjury, I declare that I have examined this return, including accompanying schedules and statements, and to the best of my knowledge and belief it is true, correct, and complete. If prepared by a person other than taxpayer, this declaration is based on all information of which the preparer has any knowledge.

Sign here ▶

Signature of fiduciary or officer representing fiduciary   Date

▶ Signature of preparer other than fiduciary (and employer's name)   Date

Identifying number (see instructions)   Address and ZIP code

Form 1041 (1976) Page 2

Schedule A.—DEPRECIATION—(See the Instructions for Schedule A for information on the depreciation methods.)

a. Description of property	b. Date acquired	c. Cost or other basis	d. Depreciation allowed or allowable in prior years	e. Method of computing depreciation	f. Life or rate	g. Depreciation for this year
1 Total additional first-year depreciation—estates only (do not include in items below) →						
2 Other depreciation: Land	1-1-76	50,000.00				
Office Building	1-1-76	100,000.00	-0-	SL	2%	2,000.00
3 Totals		150,000.00				2,000.00
4 Less amount of depreciation claimed elsewhere on return						
5 Balance (line 3 minus line 4)						2,000.00
6 Fiduciary's portion of line 5. Enter here and on page 1, line 12						492.00

Schedule B.—CHARITABLE DEDUCTION—(Attach statement giving name and address of charitable organization.)

1 Amounts paid or permanently set aside for charitable purposes from current year's income		3,920.00
2 Tax-exempt interest allocable to charitable distribution	365.00	
(Complete lines 3 and 4 below only if gain on Schedule D (Form 1041) line 15, column 2, exceeds loss on Schedule D (Form 1041) line 14, column 2.)		
3 a Long-term capital gain included on line 1		
(Do not complete lines b and c if such amounts are greater than line a)		
b Enter gain on Schedule D (Form 1041) line 15, column 2, minus loss on Schedule D (Form 1041) line 14, column 2		
c Enter gain on Schedule D (Form 1041) line 15, column 3, minus loss on Schedule D (Form 1041) line 14, column 3		
4 Enter 50% of the smallest of line 3a, line 3b, or line 3c (See instructions.)		
5 Enter sum of line 2 and line 4		365.00
6 Balance (line 1 minus line 5)		3,555.00
7 Enter short-term capital gains and 50% of the long-term capital gains of the current taxable year allocable to corpus, paid or permanently set aside for charitable purposes		
8 Amounts paid or permanently set aside for charitable purposes other than from income of the current year		
9 Total (line 6 plus lines 7 and 8). Enter here and on page 1, line 13		3,555.00

Schedule C.—DISTRIBUTABLE NET INCOME AND DISTRIBUTIONS DEDUCTION

1 Enter amount from page 1, line 16	1	36,046.00
2 Add: a Tax-exempt interest (as adjusted)	2a	3,542.00
b Net gain shown on Schedule D (Form 1041) line 16, column 1. If net loss, enter zero	2b	
c Schedule B, lines 4 and 7	2c	
d Short-term capital gain included on Schedule B, line 1	2d	
e If amount on page 1, line 6, is a loss, enter amount here as a positive figure	2e	
3 Total (line 1 through line 2e)	3	39,588.00
4 If amount on page 1, line 6, is a gain, enter amount here	4	5,000.00
5 Distributable net income (line 3 minus line 4)	5	34,588.00
6 Amount of income required to be distributed currently	6	17,640.00
7 Other amounts paid, credited, or otherwise required to be distributed	7	8,000.00
8 Total (lines 6 and 7)	8	25,640.00
9 Enter the total of tax-exempt income included on lines 6 and 7 (as adjusted)	9	2,625.00
10 Balance (line 8 minus line 9)	10	23,015.00
11 Enter distributable net income (line 5, above)	11	34,588.00
12 Enter the amount from line 2a, above	12	3,542.00
13 Balance (line 11 minus line 12)	13	31,046.00
14 Distributions deduction. Enter here and on page 1, line 17, the lesser of line 10 or line 13 above	14	23,015.00

	Yes	No		Yes	No
1 Date trust was created or, if an estate, date of decedent's death. 1-1-76			6 If a trust, was there an accumulation distribution during the year? If "Yes," attach Schedule J (Form 1041)		x
2 Did you receive tax-exempt income?	x		7 State number of Schedule(s) K-1 (Form 1041), or substitute form, attached ▶ 2		
If "Yes," did you deduct any expenses allocable to it?		x	8 Is this the final return?		x
3 If the estate or trust received income from a nominee, state name, identifying number, and address of nominee ▶			9 Did the estate or trust, at any time during the taxable year, have any interest in or signature or other authority over a bank, securities, or other financial account in a foreign country (except in a U.S. military banking facility operated by a U.S. financial institution)? If "Yes," attach Form 4683. (For definitions, see Form 4683.)		x
4 If a complex trust, is this a section 663(b) election? If "Yes," state amount ▶		x	10 Was the estate or trust the grantor of, or transferor to, a foreign trust during any taxable year, whether or not the estate or trust has any beneficial interest in such trust? If "Yes," attach Form 4683. (For definitions, see Form 4683.)		x
5 If a trust, is any section 644 tax due? If "Yes," state amount ▶ and attach computation.					

164   A CASE STUDY ILLUSTRATED

SCHEDULE D (Form 1041)
Department of the Treasury
Internal Revenue Service

Capital Gains and Losses

1976

Name of estate or trust	Employer identification number
Robert Madison Trust	65-0427191

Part I — Short-term Capital Gains and Losses—Assets Held Not More Than 6 Months

a. Kind of property and description (Example, 100 shares of "Z" Co.)	b. Date acquired (mo., day, yr.)	c. Date sold (mo., day, yr.)	d. Gross sales price	e. Cost or other basis, as adjusted, and expense of sale	f. Gain or (loss) (d less e)
1					

2 Enter net short-term gain or (loss) from partnerships and other fiduciaries … | 2 |
3 Net gain or (loss), combine lines 1 and 2 … | 3 |
4 Short-term capital loss carryover **(Attach computation)** … | 4 ( ) |
5 Net short-term gain or (loss), combine lines 3 and 4. Enter here and on line 14 below … | 5 |

Part II — Long-term Capital Gains and Losses—Assets Held More Than 6 Months

6 1,000 Sh. White Industries	1-20-76	9-16-76	90,000.00	85,000.00	5,000.00

7 Capital gain dividends … | 7 |
8 Enter gain, if applicable, from Form 4797 line 4(a)(1) … | 8 |
9 Enter net long-term gain or (loss) from partnerships and other fiduciaries … | 9 |
10 Enter net long-term gain from small business corporations (subchapter S) … | 10 |
11 Net gain or (loss), combine lines 6 through 10 … | 11 |
12 Long-term capital loss carryover **(Attach computation)** … | 12 ( ) |
13 Net long-term gain or (loss), combine lines 11 and 12. Enter here and on line 15 below … | 13 | 5,000.00 |

Part III — Summary of Parts I and II

	1. Beneficiaries	2. Fiduciary	3. Total
14 Net short-term gain or (loss) from line 5, above			
15 Net long-term gain or (loss) from line 13, above		5,000.00	5,000.00
16 Total net gain or (loss)		5,000.00	5,000.00

Enter on Form 1041, page 1, line 6, the net gain shown on line 16, column 3, above. If net (loss) on line 16, column 3, above, enter as (loss) on Form 1041, page 1, line 6, the amount computed on line 18b.

Computation of Capital Gains Deduction

17 a Long-term capital gain shown on line 15, column 3, above … | 17a | 5,000.00 |
b Short-term capital loss shown on line 14, column 3, above … | 17b ( ) |
c Excess of line 17a over line 17b, above … | 17c | 5,000.00 |
d Long-term capital gains taxable to beneficiaries. (Total of line 3 amounts from all separate Schedules K–1 (Form 1041)) | 17d |
e Balance (line 17c minus line 17d). (Enter 50% of this amount on Form 1041, page 1, line 20) … | 17e | 5,000.00 |

Computation of Capital Loss Limitation

18 Attach a computation if losses are shown on both lines 12 and 13 which are the result of a long-term capital loss carryover from years beginning before 1970, enter the amount on line 18a and note "Computation attached"; see Part IV of your retained copy of the 1975 Schedule D (Form 1041). Otherwise,
a Enter one of the following amounts:
  i If amount on line 14, column 3 is zero or a net gain, enter 50% of amount on line 16, column 3;
  ii If amount on line 15, column 3 is zero or a net gain, enter amount on line 16, column 3; or,
  iii If amounts on line 14, column 3 and line 15, column 3 are net losses, enter amount on line 14, column 3 added to 50% of amount on line 15, column 3 … | 18a |

b Enter here and enter as a (loss) on Form 1041, page 1, line 6, the smallest of:
  i The amount on line 18a;
  ii $1,000; or,
  iii Taxable income computed without regard to capital gains and losses and the deduction for exemption … | 18b ( ) |

Note: Enter the capital loss carryover to 1977:

	Pre 1970	Post 1969
Short-term …		
Long-term …		

SCHEDULE K–1 (Form 1041) Department of the Treasury Internal Revenue Service	**Beneficiary's Share of Income, Deductions, Credits, etc.—1976** for the calendar year 1976, or fiscal year beginning ...., 1976, ending ...., 19...... (Complete for each beneficiary—see instructions on back of Copy C and the instructions for Form 1041)	**Copy A** File with Form 1041

(a) Allocable share item	(b) Amount	(c) Form 1040 filers enter column (b) amount as indicated below
1 Dividends (amount before exclusion)		Schedule B, Part I, line 1
2 Short-term capital gain		Schedule D, line 2
3 Long-term capital gain		Schedule D, line 9
4 a Other taxable income (Itemize)___Net Rents___	6,534.00	
b _____Interest_____	11,094.00	
c Total of lines 4a and 4b	17,628.00	
d Depreciation and depletion (See Sch. A (1041) instrs.) . . .	1,002.00	
e Amortization deductions (Itemize) (See 1041 instr. 14.) _____		
f _____		
g Total of lines 4d, 4e and 4f	1,002.00	
h Line 4c minus line 4g	16,626.00	Schedule E, Part III
5 Foreign taxes (Attach schedule)		Form 1116 or Schedule A (Form 1040), line 16
6 a Other (Itemize)_____		Enter on applicable line of appropriate tax form
b		Enter on applicable line of appropriate tax form
Tax Preference Items — 7 Long-term capital gain		See Form 4625 Instructions
8 Depreciation (real property)		Form 4625, line 1(b) (2)
9 Depletion		Form 4625, line 1(j)
10 a Other (Itemize)_____		Enter on applicable line of Form 4625
b		Enter on applicable line of Form 4625

Name, identifying number, and address (including ZIP code) of beneficiary

338-10-7371
James Madison
1612 Belleview Ave.
Anderson, Ill. 60642

Name and employer identification number of estate or trust and name and address (including ZIP code) of fiduciary

65-0427191
Robert Madison Trust, Harry Douglas, Tr.
206 Madison Building
Anderson, Ill. 60642

SCHEDULE K–1 (Form 1041) Department of the Treasury Internal Revenue Service	**Beneficiary's Share of Income, Deductions, Credits, etc.—1976** for the calendar year 1976, or fiscal year beginning ...., 1976, ending ...., 19...... (Complete for each beneficiary—see instructions on back of Copy C and the instructions for Form 1041)	**Copy A** File with Form 1041

(a) Allocable share item	(b) Amount	(c) Form 1040 filers enter column (b) amount as indicated below
1 Dividends (amount before exclusion)		Schedule B, Part I, line 1
2 Short-term capital gain		Schedule D, line 2
3 Long-term capital gain		Schedule D, line 9
4 a Other taxable income (Itemize)___Net Rents___	1,997.00	
b _____Interest_____	3,390.00	
c Total of lines 4a and 4b	5,387.00	
d Depreciation and depletion (See Sch. A (1041) instrs.) . . .	306.00	
e Amortization deductions (Itemize) (See 1041 instr. 14.) _____		
f _____		
g Total of lines 4d, 4e and 4f	306.00	
h Line 4c minus line 4g	5,081.00	Schedule E, Part III
5 Foreign taxes (Attach schedule)		Form 1116 or Schedule A (Form 1040), line 16
6 a Other (Itemize)_____		Enter on applicable line of appropriate tax form
b		Enter on applicable line of appropriate tax form
Tax Preference Items — 7 Long-term capital gain		See Form 4625 Instructions
8 Depreciation (real property)		Form 4625, line 1(b) (2)
9 Depletion		Form 4625, line 1(j)
10 a Other (Itemize)_____		Enter on applicable line of Form 4625
b		Enter on applicable line of Form 4625

Name, identifying number, and address (including ZIP code) of beneficiary

427-01-7576
Eleanor Madison
627 Washington Ave.
Anderson, Ill. 60642

Name and employer identification number of estate or trust and name and address (including ZIP code) of fiduciary

65-0427191
Robert Madison Trust, Harry Douglas, Tr.
206 Madison Building
Anderson, Ill. 60642

Form **1041-A** (Rev. Oct. 1972) Department of the Treasury Internal Revenue Service	U.S. Information Return **Trust Accumulation of Charitable, etc., Amounts** For calendar year 19 76, or fiscal year beginning , 19 , and ending , 19	

Name of trust Robert Madison Trust	Employer identification number 65-0427191

Name of fiduciary   Harry Douglas, Trustee

Address of fiduciary (Number and street)   206 Madison Building

City or town, State, and ZIP code   Anderson, Ill.   60642

◀ Part I ▶ Income

1 Dividends		
2 Interest	24,000	00
3 Income from partnerships and other fiduciaries		
4 Gross rents and royalties	15,000	00
5 Gross profit (loss) from trade or business		
6 Net gain (loss) from capital assets	5,000	00
7 Ordinary gains and (losses)		
8 Other income (state nature of income)		
9 Total gross income (lines 1 to 8 inclusive)	44,000	00
Deductions		
10 Interest		
11 Taxes		
12 Trustee's portion of depreciation and depletion	492	00
13 Charitable deduction	3,555	00
14 Other expenses (itemize): Rent Expenses 3,000; Administrative Expenses 907.00	3,907	00
15 Total expenses and charitable deduction (lines 10 to 14, inclusive)	7,954	00
16 Gross income less expenses and charitable deduction (line 9 less line 15)	36,046	00

◀ Part II ▶ Charitable, Etc., Contributions Paid From Prior Years' Income or Principal (See Instruction 6)

List in 1(b) and 2(b) the purposes for which disbursements were made and the total amount for each purpose

1 Charitable, etc., deductions taken but not paid out in prior years under section 642(c) of Code:

(a) Total not paid out at beginning of this taxable year			-0-
(b) Paid out during this taxable year			
(c) Not paid out at end of taxable year (item (a) less item (b))			-0-

2 Paid out of principal for charitable, etc., purposes:

(a) Paid out in prior years			
(b) Paid out within this taxable year			
			-0-

GLOSSARY

ACCUMULATION DISTRIBUTION. A current year's distribution from a trust which consists of income earned and accumulated in prior years.

ADMINISTRATION. The management of property placed in trust, including the payment of expenses and distributions, and the rendition of proper accounts.

ALTERNATE TRUSTEE. A person named to serve as trustee in the event the person first named is unable or unwilling to serve.

APPRAISE. To establish cost or value by systematic procedures that include physical examination, pricing, and often engineering estimates.

BENEFICIAL INTEREST. An interest in property held in trust, as distinguished from legal ownership.

BENEFICIARY. One who is lawfully entitled to the proceeds of property, the title to which is vested in another, such as an executor or trustee.

BUSINESS TRUST. A form of organization, having many of the characteristics of a trust, for carrying on a joint venture or business operation.

CHARGE AND DISCHARGE STATEMENT. A tabular summary prepared for an executor, administrator, trustee, or other fiduciary, accounting for the principal and income for which he has been responsible and constituting a part of an interim or final report on his activities.

CONDUIT PRINCIPLE. An income tax principle meaning that income earned by a fiduciary retains the same character in the hands of a beneficiary to whom it is distributed that it had in the hands of the fiduciary.

CORPUS. The property comprising the fund which has been set aside in trust, or from which income is expected to accrue; principal.

CREATOR. The person who establishes a trust, either while alive or through will on death.

DEDUCTION FOR DISTRIBUTIONS. The deduction allowed on a fiduciary income tax return for income currently paid, credited, or required to be distributed to beneficiaries.

DISCRETIONARY TRUST. A trust in which the trustee is given the power to use his discretion in connection with certain stipulated acts.

DISTRIBUTABLE NET INCOME. For fiduciary income tax purposes, the taxable income of the trust for a year, computed with certain modifications.

EXPRESS TRUST. A trust created by specific provision in a deed or other written instrument.

FIDUCIARY. Any person responsible for the custody or administration, or both, of property belonging to another; as, a trustee, executor, or administrator.

FIDUCIARY ACCOUNTING. The preparation and keeping of accounts for property in the hands of a trustee, executor, or administrator, whether under the direct jurisdiction of a court or acting by virtue of a deed of trust, will, or other instrument of appointment.

FIDUCIARY ACCOUNTING INCOME. The net income of a trust as determined by any specific directions in the trust instrument or by state law, without regard to income tax rules.

GRANTOR. The person who established a trust; creator; settlor.

GRANTOR TRUST. A trust which fails to meet certain income tax rules and the property of which is, therefore, considered to be still owned by the grantor for income tax purposes.

IMPLIED TRUST. A trust where the intent of the parties to create a trust is inferred from the transaction between them.

INCOME BENEFICIARY. The person entitled to the income from property in trust, as contrasted with a principal beneficiary, who will receive the property itself.

INTER-VIVOS TRUST. A trust created between living persons, as contrasted with a testamentary trust.

IRREVOCABLE TRUST. A trust that cannot be set aside by its creator.

LIFE ESTATE. The title of the interest owned by the life tenant, income beneficiary.

LIFE TENANT. The person who receives the income from a legal life estate or from a trust fund during his own life or that of another person.

LIVING TRUST. A trust created by a living person, to take effect before his death; an inter-vivos trust.

MARITAL DEDUCTION TRUST. A testamentary trust which meets certain tax requirements so that its property may qualify for the marital deduction.

PERSONAL PROPERTY. Property of a temporary and movable character as contrasted with real property.

PRINCIPAL. The original amount of a trust fund together with accretions which may, but usually do not, include income.

PRINCIPAL BENEFICIARY. The person to whom the property constituting the principal of a trust will go upon termination of the trust.

REAL PROPERTY. Land and land improvements, including buildings and appurtenances.

REMAINDERMAN. One entitled to the corpus or principal of a trust upon the expiration of a prior estate, such as a life tenancy.

REVOCABLE TRUST. A trust terminable at the pleasure of, or under certain conditions by, its creator.

SETTLOR. The person who makes a gift to an inter-vivos trust.

SHORT-TERM TRUST. A trust established to be irrevocable for a period of at least ten years; also known as a "Clifford" trust.

SUCCESSOR TRUSTEE. One named to assume the duties of trustee upon the death or disqualification of the original trustee.

TESTAMENTARY TRUST. A trust created by a person's will.

TESTATOR. One who makes a will.

TRUST. A right, enforceable in courts of equity, to the beneficial enjoyment of property, the legal title to which is in another. The person creating the trust is the creator, settlor, grantor, or donor; the holder of the legal title is the trustee; and the holder of the beneficial interest is the beneficiary.

TRUST—COMPLEX. For income tax purposes, all trusts other than "simple" trusts.

TRUST—SIMPLE. For income tax purposes a trust which requires that income, as defined by the governing instrument or by local law, be distributed currently to the beneficiaries other than charities.

TRUST FUND. A fund held by one person, the trustee, for the benefit of another, pursuant to the provisions of a formal trust agreement.

TRUST RES. The property placed in trust.

TRUSTEE. The fiduciary nominated by the testator or settlor or appointed by the court to administer the trust property.

TRUSTOR. A person who established a trust; creator; grantor.

TRUST INSTRUMENT. A written document reciting the terms and conditions under which property placed in trust shall be adminstered.

INDEX

175